Meanness Mania

MEANNESS MANIA
The Changed Mood

By Gerald R. Gill

Institute for the Study of Educational Policy
Howard University

Published for ISEP by
HOWARD UNIVERSITY PRESS
Washington, D.C.
1980

Library of Congress Cataloging in Publication Data

Gill, Gerald R.   1948–
  Meanness Mania.

  Bibliography: p.
  Includes index.
  1. Afro-Americans—Education. 2. Afro-Americans—Employment. 3. United States—Race relations. 4. Conservatism—United States. 5. Affirmative action programs.
  I. Howard University, Washington, D.C. Institute for the Study of Educational Policy.
  II. Title.
LC2717.G54   305.8′00973   79-27400
ISBN 0-88258-081-7
ISBN 0-88258-082-5 pbk.

This report was made possible by a grant from the Ford Foundation.

Contents

List of Tables and Figures   vii

Foreword   ix

1 Overview   1

2 The Conservative/ Neo-Conservative Impulse   14

3 The Great Society Assessed   18

4 Black Progress: Myths and Realities   25

5 Attacks on American Public Education   36

6 The Opposition to Busing   41

7 Tuition Tax Credits and Education Vouchers   47

8 Competency Based Testing   54

9 Proposition 13 and the Tax Revolt   57

10 Affirmative Action:
Bakke and *Weber* Cases   63

Afterword   71

Appendix:
Justice Marshall on *Bakke* Decision   75

Notes   85

Index   97

List of Tables and Figures

Figure   *Page*

1 Selected Examples of Black Economic and
   Social Progress, 1970–1977   27

2 Black and White Unemployment, 1967–1978   28

3 Black Income as a Percentage of White
   Income, 1965–1978   30

Table

1 Minority Presence on Selected Newspaper Staffs   33

2 College Costs *vs.* Family Income   48

3 Comparative Percentage of Government Spending   58

Foreword

The Institute for the Study of Educational Policy (ISEP) is the outgrowth of a serious effort by educators and foundations to establish a commission on the higher education of black Americans.* Beginning with a series of substantial grants from the Ford Foundation to Howard University, ISEP started small-scale operations in March, 1974 and full-scale operations in October, 1974. The Institute's mandate is to act as a national clearinghouse for data and a research center on the issues affecting equal opportunity for blacks in higher education. Through its reports and monographs, through its seminars and workshops, and through its announcements and public testimony, ISEP seeks to fill a vacuum in the organized body of knowledge on minority participation in higher education. In pursuit of its second program objective, to monitor and evaluate the impact of law, social science and other research on the status and situation of blacks in higher education, ISEP hopes to make a significant contribution to the formulation and evaluation of contemporary educational policy to assist the public and private sectors in responding to the socio-economic factors which either facilitate or impede equal educational opportunity.

The National Advisory Board of the Institute at its first meeting in June, 1974 expressed grave concern regarding a changing mood in the United States. This mood seemed to indicate that the country was reducing its strong commitment to justice and equity for blacks and other oppressed minorities. A number of themes espoused by neo-conservatives circulated in society which expressed this changing mood. Among these themes were the claims that socio-economic problems were intractable and subject to haphazard forces such that government could ac-

---

*On December 3, 1968, the then President of Cornell University, Dr. James A. Perkins, in a speech before the United Negro College Fund stated:

> The time has come to raise the question as to whether or not a *National Commission on Higher Education for the Negro* is not a long overdue necessity. It seems to me that the problem of higher education for the Negro is clearly a national problem and requires a careful and systematic examination of all the barriers that still exist to achieving our two ultimate objectives. The first must be to have the same percentage of Black students in higher education as there are Black students in the age group. . . . And the second objective must be that . . . the educational opportunities to the talented Black student must be of equivalent quality to those available to the white students. (Emphasis added)

complish more by doing less; educational inputs such as faculty, curricula, and facilities had no substantial correlation with educational outputs such as academic achievement and performance; and blacks were genetically inferior to whites in native intelligence.

The Board advised the staff to study this changing mood which resulted in the publication of *The Changing Mood in America: Eroding Commitment?* by Dr. Faustine Jones, who served as a Senior Fellow on the staff of the Institute from August, 1974 through May, 1977. Dr. Jones having documented the changing mood, the Board further advised the staff to call a national conference in which the anti-affirmative action expressions of the changing mood could be dealt with. The transcript of the proceedings of that conference were published in 1978 in a volume entitled *Advancing Equality of Opportunity: A Matter of Justice,* edited by Dr. Cynthia J. Smith, a former Visiting Senior Fellow at the Institute. Since the publication of *The Changing Mood* and *Advancing Equality of Opportunity,* the Board agreed that the issues and the problems dealt with in both publications needed further elucidation because it appeared that the mood of the country was no longer changing but had changed. Thus, Gerald Gill, a former Research Fellow on the staff on the Institute, was assigned the task of updating the research and analysis carried out in *The Changing Mood.* The product of his contemporary historical review is this volume which has the subtitle *The Changed Mood.*

This monograph is an important commentary on the current developments in the social, political, cultural and economic affairs of the United States. Policy formulation cannot take place in a vacuum. If the Institute is to assist realistically in providing the information and analysis that policymakers and decisionmakers in our country need to make better decisions and to formulate better policies, it must make clear what social, political, cultural and economic currents condition and constrain decisionmaking and policymaking. Mr. Gill shows that there is in fact a changed mood which expresses itself-in fiscal and social conservatism. Fiscal and social conservatism are further expressed in certain social, political, and cultural themes and trends. These are an indifference and antipathy to the plight of blacks and other oppressed groups; preoccupation with self or, what might be called, "cultural narcissism" or social solipsism; and fear of economic uncertainty. Specifically, the above socio-economic factors have resulted in opposition to affirmative action, the middle-class tax revolt, attacks on busing to achieve integration, a retrenchment from domestic efforts to improve the lot of the deprived and disadvantaged and a call for the escalation of military budgets for dealing with external concerns. Although Mr. Gill states that economic discontent and inflation probably best explain the advent of what he calls the "meanness mania," he thinks strong credence should be given "to the cyclical theory of the ebb and flow of liberalism *via-a-vis* conservatism." However, that there has been an ebb and flow of public policy in the last fifty years cannot be gainsaid.

The ebb and flow of national policy have given rise to eight national administrations which can be characterized by eight catch phrases: the New Deal of President Franklin D. Roosevelt, the Fair Deal of President Harry S. Truman, the Stand-Pat Deal of President Dwight D. Eisenhower, the New Frontier of President John F. Kennedy, the Great Society of President Lyndon B. Johnson, the Neo-conservative Deal of President Richard Milhous Nixon, and the WINning Deal of President Gerald R. Ford, and the Born-Again Populism of President Jimmy Carter.

Each of the above administrations in its own way confronted poverty and minority problems. The first could not have confronted society at all without confronting poverty because of the Great Depression. The second planted seeds of hope and concern for the despised and the infirm. The third confronted poverty by turning its back on the present and facing the past. The fourth confronted it by creating a Camelot of elegance, style and taste—while gracefully traversing the new frontier of art, drama, and the arrestingly eloquent pronouncement. President Johnson perpetuated the tradition of FDR, brought to bloom the seeds of HST, reversed the stance of IKE, and gave substance to the style and grace of JFK. In short, in the midst of plenty and affluence, President Johnson declared war on poverty, racism and ignorance. Thus, he achieved an explosion of social legislation in the Economic Opportunity Act of 1964; the Civil Rights Act of 1964, the Voting Rights Act of 1965, and the Fair Housing Act of 1968; and the Elementary and Secondary Education Act and the Higher Education Act, both of 1965. However, President Johnson's great domestic achievements were flawed by the Vietnam War imbroglio which ultimately sacrificed butter for guns, curdling the economy with the inevitable smell of inflation. President Nixon's election in 1968 was a thinly disguised backlash against the reformist commitment, particularly of President Johnson, to advance blacks, and the campus and civil disturbances over Vietnam and ghetto discontents.

It took some time for the positive momentum of the Great Society and the sixties to slow down, but slow down it did as Mr. Gill chronicles. It may be worth considering whether the slow down was primarily a product of backlash or a displacement of the civil rights movement with the ecology, consumer, gay, handicapped, and feminist movements. President Nixon nearly wrecked the ship of state on the shoals of Watergate, and President Ford pardoned him. Finally, President Carter ran for government against government, exuding a born-again populism which is both ingratiating and irritating. In large measure, the changing mood which began in the late sixties and ran through the middle seventies became the changed mood during the first three years of the presidential term of the very decent and intelligent peanut-farmer governor from Georgia.

The changed mood which Mr. Gill describes makes clear the changes in fashions of thought and policies. Hopefully, Mr. Gill's lucid description of the changed mood will operate like the change in styles of swim suits: the more they reveal the facts of life, the more the country will become interested in and stimulated to face and deal with those facts. However, the flesh of the body politic which Gill reveals is blotched with the pimples and scars of self-indulgent adolescence and inflated with the flab of stultified affluence.

Neo-conservative intellectuals and pundits proclaim that government is "overloaded" because it is trying to do too much domestically, yet they also claim that it is not doing enough militarily and internationally. They advocate "lowered expectations" and the facile acceptance of the *status quo*.

Notwithstanding, neo-conservatives are jaded and unnerved by the difficulty of past and present efforts to reform and improve society. Gill shows in an assessment of the Great Society that reform accomplished much. For example, between 1965 and 1969 the number of black Americans living in poverty decreased 25 percent; whites, 43 percent, although poverty programs were underfunded, not over-funded. In 1966, $30 billion were spent on Vietnam, three times the amount allocated to the Office of Economic Opportunity between 1965–1970. Head Start and many other Great Society programs, particularly those concerned with expanding higher educational opportunity for the poor, blacks, and other minorities, enjoyed much more success than they have been given credit for.

However, although the Great Society and the programs it initiated accomplished much, Gill shows whites incorrectly believe that blacks have made a great deal more progress than they have actually made and "that blacks are no longer the victims of discrimination." Gill shows with graphic tables and statistics that "... at best, the progress made by blacks has been *uneven* and *inconsistent*, determined to a great extent by the state of the economy." An example of unevenness and inconsistency, if not discrimination, is that white high school dropouts experience a rate of unemployment which is less than that of blacks who have graduated from high school or even attended college. Moreover, highly educated blacks who constitute most of the black families which enjoy incomes over $25,202—"the budget level for higher standard of living"—have lost ground between 1972–77. The proportion of black families enjoying such a higher standard of living dropped to 9 percent in 1977 from 12 percent in 1972.

Although education together with a thriving economy is essential for black progress, Gill shows that there has been an "open season" on public schools recently. This seems to be less than a happenstance since blacks are attending inner-city public schools in larger numbers. Busing to effect integration has been excoriated by many, yet it is being done with less violence and with a significant measure of educational success.

Society has not contented itself with just an open season on public schools and attacks upon busing now that so many blacks attend public schools. Presently, there is a revival of interest in tuition tax credits and educational vouchers, proposals which, if fully implemented, would undermine public schools further and slow the movement toward equal opportunity in higher education. These proposals obviously would disproportionately benefit whites who could afford to send their children to private and expensive schools. Both proposals are products of false perceptions of the ravages of fortunes affluent whites are experiencing. Between 1967 and 1976, for example, college cost has increased less than family income. Thus, college cost as a percentage of family median income has actually gone down. Therefore, Gill correctly observes that there are "substantial differences between ability and willingness of parents to pay for the costs of college education." The prime beneficiaries of tuition tax credits are upper-income families who need assistance least. The question of education vouchers, Gill shows, is "a more radical extension of the tuition tax credit argument." There is little evidence that it will serve well any public purpose.

As if the "open season" on public schools, attacks on busing, and tuition tax credits and educational vouchers were not enough to undermine the education position of blacks and the poor, now comes competency based testing, at a time when standardized tests are being questioned, to resegregate blacks through classroom tracking within schools which have been desegregated.

If the above do not do grievous harm to blacks and the poor, Proposition 13 and the tax revolt surely will. Yet, Gill shows conclusively that government spending and taxation are low in the United States compared with other affluent Western countries. Gill maintains that Proposition 13 or the tax revolt "should be viewed as an expression and manifestation of narrow individual and class interests, motivated in large part by greed and race." Proposition 13 lowered property taxes in California which means almost by definition it was principally for the benefit of the affluent.

Gill ends his chronicle of the changed mood by discussing affirmative action programs in education and employment. It is a melancholy climax to a seamy series of tales about selfishness, greed, and insensitivity or indifference to the situation of the poor, blacks, and other oppressed groups. The colorable issues of principle involved in affirmative action programs become very questionable when they are placed in the context of the earlier enumeration of indifference or antipathy, preoccupation with self, and fear and insecurity about the economy. Affirmative action has helped blacks in the past. Attacks on it in the courts, particularly the *Bakke* case, appear to have had some chilling effect upon black enrollment in graduate and professional schools. *Bakke* provides a thin shaft of light in its recognition of the legitimacy of taking race into account in the admissions process, and the *Weber* case provides even a brighter ray of hope in its upholding of affirmative action in employment to correct societal discrimination.

It is peculiarly appropriate that Gill's chronicle ends with the discussion of a subject which definitely has a bright side, for surely the National Advisory Board in directing this study to be done was motivated by a desire to light a candle rather than curse the darkness in public policy. Indeed, the underlying assumption and conviction which fuel and motivate the operation of ISEP are that there is a reservoir of decency in the United States such that if the facts of discrimination, meanness, and selfishness are made clear, the public will respond positively, rationally, and generously. Moreover, the issue of displacement was not fully or substantially explored in this monograph which means that the dispersion of energy, resources, and goodwill to deal with the problems of the environment, consumer protection, women's rights, ageing, and the handicapped may express more a psychological need to enconomize in commitments than a "meanness mania." In any case, the Board did not ask Gill to deal with the displacement question, and what he was directed to do he has done well, and the Board is grateful to him. Many members of the Board do not necessarily endorse the term, "meanness mania," but they unanimously recognize a changed mood in the country. Furthermore, the Board hopes that this short monograph will revive a mood of concern and commitment to public policies which will advance the common good by promoting equality of educational opportunity for blacks, the poor, and other oppressed groups.

Finally, Howard University and the Institute gratefully acknowledge the substantial and continued support of the Ford Foundation.

Kenneth S. Tollett
Chairman
National Advisory Board
Institute for the Study of
Educational Policy

January 1980

Meanness Mania

1

Overview

The past several years, from 1977 to the present, have revealed a clear shift in the attitudes of members of Congress, many leading intellectuals and much of the American public toward both social welfare programs and strategies designed to improve the lives and livelihoods of blacks, other minorities and the poor. In the 1960s the federal government and the larger society made commitments to better the conditions of impoverished Americans and to strive to eliminate the formal and informal barriers to racial equality. Now, less than twenty years later, there has arisen a *changed* mood and attitude toward such programs and strategies. Instead of compassion, one witnesses hostility toward efforts to reduce economic inequities and to overcome the effects of past and present discrimination. Instead of appeals to achieve equal educational and economic opportunities, one hears code words like "forced busing", "white flight" and "reverse discrimination." These code words are manifestations of a spreading mania within American society, a mania increasingly adamant against governmental and societal efforts to help blacks, other minorities and the poor. It is not too much to suggest that behind this mania is a growing feeling of meanness. While "meanness" is a strong categorization, it is an apt one to explain the current mood among much of the American populace. For "meanness" denotes selfishness, stinginess and malice. As is apparently more evident during the late 1970s, these denotations—selfishness, stinginess and malice—are expressions of an increasing unwillingness and hostility upon the part of many citizens to share more equally the benefits of American society.

This brief monograph is an attempt to explore and to counterattack the increasing number of arguments against societal and governmental efforts to ensure equal opportunity for blacks and similarly situated groups—other

1

minorities and the poor. In the past several years much scholarly and lay literature produced by neo–conservative and conservative scholars has questioned and has criticized heavily the need for further and, in some cases, continued governmental and societal efforts in behalf of the disadvantaged. The thrust of much of this literature is aimed rather pointedly at the alleged shortcomings and failures of the "Great Society" programs and at the alleged disruptive and injurious effects of such programs as affirmative action in education and in employment, and at such strategies as busing.

This monograph reviews and responds to these arguments and concerns. It purports to show the concrete benefits that such programs and strategies bring to individuals and to the larger society. Individual gains have been realized from programs as varied as Head Start, Job Corps, busing, special minority admissions programs and affirmative action programs. As a whole, these programs translate into benefits, both immediate and long term, for the larger society. Neo-conservative scholars are prone to analyze issues in terms of a cost-benefit analysis in which they ask, "do the benefits outweigh the costs?" This volume asks, "are the benefits to individuals and to society worth the costs?" If equal educational and economic opportunity are to be attained, the answer is a resounding "Yes".

Having examined the racial attitudes and behavior of white Americans from 1969 through 1975, Dr. Faustine C. Jones concluded that there was a *changing mood*, one of increasing conservatism adrift in the nation. This new mood, she observed, was "more negative than positive" with regard to its attitudes and practices toward blacks, other minorities and the poor.[1] However, the three years that have elapsed since the cut-off date for Jones' study have been marked by a *changed* mood, one in which fiscal and social conservatism are not only increasing but have become the dominant political, cultural, and social trends of the late 1970s. Three socio-economic factors help to explain this new mood of conservatism:

1. an increased indifference and antipathy, at times hostility, toward societal and governmental programs on behalf of blacks, other minorities and the poor;

2. a general preoccupation among many Americans with individual concerns and interests; and,

3. a growing fear of economic uncertainty, sparked by the spiraling inflation rate.

Increasingly, both news accounts and magazine articles, some warily and others gleefully, point to a rightward shift in the thoughts and attitudes of the American populace.[2] As indicators of this trend, these articles cite mounting instances of a growing conservatism on domestic issues and an increased *hawkishness* on foreign policy concerns. This rising domestic conservatism expresses itself in the growing opposition to government-sponsored and supported legislation, regulations and court decisions. Evidence of this social conservatism is exemplified by the opposition to affirmative action programs, government spending for social welfare programs, busing, and the Equal Rights Amendment. At the same time, this conservatism encourages government intervention via legislation to curtail abortions, restore the death penalty and restrict the rights of homosexuals. Evidence of the increased *hawkishness* in foreign policy is the demand for a more "hardline" foreign policy toward the Soviet Union, and a reassertion of American military and diplomatic strength. Exemplifying this return to the "big-stick" posture are calls for an increase in defense spending, the resumption of the draft, the lifting of sanctions against Zimbabwe-Rhodesia, the opposition to the SALT II Treaty, and the continued opposition to the Panama Canal Treaty.

This conservatism, increasingly evident over the course of the past two to three years, has emerged to a large degree during the Carter administration. While his administration has not overtly encouraged this attitude, the increasing fiscal conservatism of the administration is, in part, a response to the mood. After two and one half years of the Carter presidency, one witnessed a governmental retreat from the New Deal, Fair Deal, New Frontier, Great Society themes of his Democratic predecessors. Whereas Lyndon Johnson could state that the role of government "is to make it possible for all citizens to experience a better, more secure, and more rewarding life," the Carter administration counsels Americans that "life is unfair" or that the present era is the era of "new realities."[3]

Two domestic trends particularly reflective of these realities are the continuing opposition to affirmative action programs in education and in employment, as evidenced by the *Bakke* and *Weber* cases, and the middle-class tax revolt, as evidenced by the passage of Proposition 13 in California. These two trends reflect, in part, a more hardened and hostile attitude among many white Americans toward blacks, other minorities and the poor. Terming this attitude the "new negativism," Vernon Jordan of the National Urban League has sharply noted that it reflects "a national backlash against the movement toward greater economic and racial equality."[4]

While the Jordan assessment is an accurate reading of the current American mood, his argument does not go far enough in explaining this new mood. For backlash, as understood in the context of the 1960s and early 1970s, was a hostile reaction and response by lower-middle-class Americans, particularly white ethnics, to social change. However, the prime movers and supporters of the tax revolt and opponents of affirmative action have not been lower-middle-class white ethnics, but the upwardly mobile middle-class and the emerging conservative-neo-conservative intellectual bloc. A 1978 study of the American

3

mood found the strongest opposition to government spending to improve the situation of blacks, not among those considered lower-middle-class white ethnics, but among those whose family incomes exceeded $20,000 annually.[5] The support of prominent conservative economists for Proposition 13 helped to *legitimize* the initiative in the eyes of many Californians.[6] Moreover, as evidenced by the steady and seemingly unrelenting stream of literature, those most critical of affirmative action plans in education and employment, are academicians and journalists.[7] Thus, what is presently being witnessed is a phenomenon that extends beyond "Bunkerism"—the backlash of the 1960s and early 1970s. Individuals once supportive of the aims and aspirations of blacks, other minorities and the poor have emerged as the molders of this new mood and as the leaders of the new negativism. For it is these academicians and journalists who are refocusing and shifting societal and governmental concerns away from the plight of the disadvantaged toward the interests of the middle- and upper-income classes.

Nowhere has this shift been more apparent than in Congress. There is increased reluctance and hostility in both Houses of Congress, but especially in the House of Representatives, to support and maintain programs designed to aid blacks and the poor. In the past three sessions, Congress has passed three amendments to legislation, the Esch, Byrd and Eagleton-Biden amendments, in attempts to curb federal ordering or enforcement of busing. The House of Representatives has passed the Walker-Levitas and the Walker amendments, designed to weaken and curtail the current federal efforts to implement affirmative action programs in education and employment. Likewise, the House has twice passed the Hyde Amendment, designed to prevent the federal funding of abortions for the poor. And in attempts to "reduce fraud and abuse" in federal social welfare programs, Congress has focused primarily on programs such as Food Stamps, Medicaid and Aid to Families with Dependent Children. Congress' attitude toward these particular programs was revealed in its proposed threat to withhold monies for them unless fraud and waste were reduced by one billion dollars.[8] However, the real victims of this proposed attempt to "reduce fraud and abuse" would not be the administrators of these programs, but many genuinely indigent individuals and families who are dependent upon these programs. Moreover, Congress has failed to pass needed welfare reform and urban aid legislation. Perhaps the remarks of an unnamed Congressional aide best describe the current mood of Congress:

> I don't believe there's any stomach for new initiatives for the poor any more. All the innovative thought is going into new programs for the middle class. The best anybody's prepared to do for the poor is to target the existing help toward them more tightly.[9]

4

The essence of Congress' concern for the "haves" at the expense of the "have nots" can be seen in its passage last session of the tax reform bill. Under this new law, a clear departure from most tax reform legislation, most of the benefits would go to the *more* affluent rather than to the *least* affluent members of society. It is estimated that 44 percent of the benefits will go to the 5 percent of all taxpayers with adjusted gross incomes above $30,000. The real winners are the forty-nine thousand taxpayers with incomes over $200,000. For them the special provision affecting capital gains was removed and it is estimated that the average reduction in capital gains taxes will be close to $14,000 per person. Such legislation clearly benefits the upper class.[10]

How does one explain the present mood and the preoccupation with the affluent? It is a clear retreat from, if not *erosion* of, the commitment that the American people made in the 1960s, to improve the lives and livelihoods of blacks, other minorities and the poor. This retreat has been shaped and conditioned by the belief among many Americans that blacks have made considerable political, social and economic progress over the past twenty-five years. While blacks have made progress, many perceive the success of *individual* blacks, particularly those highly paid blacks in the fields of sports and entertainment, as an indication of progress for the *masses* of blacks and as a justification to reduce or to cut back programs designed for blacks.

Moreover, an increasing amount of popular and social science literature extols recent black economic progress. Sociologist William Julius Wilson's *The Declining Significance of Race* declares that class, not race, is the key factor in determining the economic life chances of individual blacks. As the title of economist Richard Barry Freeman's most recent book, *Black Elite: The New Market for Highly Educated Black Americans,* suggests, there are expanded job opportunities in both the private and public sectors for well-educated blacks.[11] Because of their preoccupation with a "black elite," these two works give the mistaken impression to many that entrance and advancement of blacks into largely heretofore closed occupations has led to the virtual elimination of racial discrimination in employment.

While that promised day has not yet arrived, the recently released Louis Harris and Associates poll reveals that the public strongly supports the view that racial discrimination in the economic sphere has all but ended. Fully underestimating the severity and impact of unemployment and underemployment on blacks, white Americans tend to regard discrimination against blacks in employment as minimal.[12]

At the same time, conservative and neo-conservative writers continue to attack those Great Society programs designed to help the less fortunate. These writers and scholars, whose ranks are growing in size and influence, advocate that the federal, state and local governments do less for the poor, particularly in the area of public assistance. One very recent work by economist Martin Anderson, entitled *Welfare: The Political Economy of Welfare Reform in the United States*, boldly asserts that the "war on poverty has been won, except for perhaps a few mopping-up operations." Hence, Anderson concludes, in the all-too-familiar neo-conservative criticism of Great Society programs, that unneeded poverty programs should be eliminated and those remaining should be made "more effective and more efficient."[13] Also, Senator S. I. Hayakawa's remarks in 1979 about the price of gasoline and the poor reveal both an insensitivity to and a callousness toward the plight of the poor, and a preoccupation with the well-being of the well-to-do. According to the Senator:

> Let the gasoline go up. If the price of gasoline rises to $2 or $2.50 or even $3 a gallon, the wealthy still would buy it . . . The important thing is that a lot of the poor don't need gasoline because they're not working. . . . The wealthy are driving around in the private jets and Cadillacs, and they're going to do that whether they have to pay 95 cents for gas or $2 to $3 for gas. That's what it means to be wealthy.[14]

Given both the mistaken public perception of the degree of black progress and the emergent intellectual/political callousness toward the poor, it is little wonder that the problems of black Americans ranked last out of thirty-one possible choices in a recently published survey of national issues by William Watts and Lloyd H. Free entitled *The State of the Union III*.[15] It is also becoming apparent that the problems of blacks and the poor are being or will soon be overshadowed by the support expressed for the nation's newest minority—the Vietnamese boat people. President Carter, members of Congress, volunteer agencies and concerned citizens, black and white, have expressed their support for the boat people. Such concern is a continuance of American humanitarianism toward refugees. Yet some of these very persons, particularly some of the members of Congress, who are so concerned with the plight of the Vietnamese boat people are blind to or opposed to the need to maintain or to continue to support programs to benefit America's "urban boat people."[16]

One marked change in the present attitudes toward blacks is the increasing attacks by members of the media, commentators and social scientists upon black leaders and black organizations. Prior to his resignation as United States Ambassador to the United Nations, Andrew Young was the repeated subject of attacks, often hostile, in newspapers and magazines.[17] Other black leaders have not been spared. Leaders of civil rights organizations, community organizations and black elected officials have been attacked on such grounds as being "too loyal" to Andrew Young, anti-Catholic, anti-Semitic and for holding views at variance with those of the black rank-and-file.[18] Yet these very same organizations and individuals so criticized today were being praised for their *moderate* views just a few years ago.[19]

But the new mood is fueled not just by racial antipathy and in some instances overt hostility, but by social indifference and economic fear. This social indifference is characterized by the present preoccupation with self, not society; with *me*, not *we*. Such inwardness is reflected in both the message and popularity of books such as *Looking Out for Number One, How to Be Your Own Best Friend,* and *How to Say No Without Feeling Guilty.* These titles aptly reflect the ethos of the 1970s, described by writer and social commentator Tom Wolfe as the "Me Decade," and more recently by historian Christopher Lasch as "The Culture of Narcissism." Wolfe contends that the post-World War II economic boom in this country has altered peoples' lives so that they "discovered and started doting on 'Me'."[20] Following up the theme of the Wolfe essay, Lasch has pessimistically observed:

> After the political turmoil of the sixties, Americans have retreated to purely personal preoccupations. Having no hope of improving their lives in any of the ways that matter, people have convinced themselves that what matters is psychic self-improvement; getting in touch with their feelings, eating health food, taking lessons in ballet or belly-dancing, immersing themselves in the wisdom of the East, jogging, learning how to "relate," overcoming the "fear of pleasure." Harmless in themselves, these pursuits, elevated to a program and wrapped in the rhetoric of authenticity and awareness, signify a retreat from politics and a repudiation of the recent past.[21]

But, if religion is the opiate of the masses, is preoccupation with self the "opiate of the upper middle class?"[22] Lasch thinks not, but other critics of "narcissism' do. Peter Marin contends that the "new narcissism" allows the affluent to overlook societal problems and concerns while fulfilling their own interests.[23] Edwin M. Schur, author of *The Awareness Trap: Self-Absorption Instead of Social Change,* offers a more biting indictment than does Marin. Schur attacks the self-fulfillment/self-satisfaction movement for addressing problems peculiar to the affluent—such as difficulties in "relating," or choosing more "creative" work—rather than the more serious societal problems of poverty and racism.[24] This is evident in recent accounts of the activities and whereabouts of the "Woodstock Generation." While several of those interviewed have retained their ideological fervor and commitment to change, others have greatly altered their life-styles and beliefs. Part of this change is reflected in the views of a former anti-war activist who now professes, "When I have time off, I'd rather play tennis than go to a march."[25]

While the self-fulfillment/self-awareness movement is an example of the affluent adrift and the changing perspective of the college-educated, economic discontent and dissatisfaction, as shown in the overriding societal and governmental concern with the problem of inflation, probably best explains what is

7

meant by "meanness mania." Benjamin Hooks, Executive Secretary of the NAACP, graphically illustrates this point:

> Inflation makes people mean, vicious and selfish. It draws them inward. People worry about can I eat? Can I buy a second car? Can I send my own child to school? They stop worrying about the black child down the street.[26]

The combination of spiraling inflation rates and slower economic growth has preoccupied the thoughts and activities of public policymakers and the majority of the American public. But this concern is usually not translated into action to those most vulnerable to the impact of inflation, those on fixed incomes, usually the elderly, the poor and blacks.

Media accounts sympathize with the plight of the "middle class poor" or "the troubled middle class."[27] However, few bother to ascertain who or what the "nouveau poor" are and just how severe their plight is compared to that of the real poor. Recent Census Bureau statistics, based upon 1977 data, provide indicators by which to define the poor: a non-farm family of four with an income of less than $6,191. No such indicator exists which defines "middle class"; estimates of who is "middle-class" vary anywhere from family incomes of $15,000 to $50,000.[28] A recent analysis of both Census Bureau and Internal Revenue Service data points out that the middle class, defined as those having yearly incomes of between $18,000 and $40,000 is both smaller and better off than is perceived by the public.[29] From 1967 through 1977, the income of the middle class has risen faster, 112 percent more than the twin horrors of the consumer price index and property taxes.[30] And even though economic growth has slowed considerably during the mid-to-late 1970s, personal income is *still* rising faster than inflation. According to figures released by the Labor Department individual income increased 11.2 percent in 1978 while the consumer price index rose nine percent.[31] While indicative of continued though moderate growth, these figures show that the incomes of most blue collar and white collar workers continue to outpace inflation.

Personal cutbacks in spending have been noted, but there are still enough indicators that the vast majority of middle-income and upper-income Americans are enjoying "the good life." There is a continued demand for housing and automobiles. And while the gas crisis of the summer of 1979 had a profound impact on the vacation plans of many, alternate modes of transportation—rail, air and bus—were discovered. The cruise industry is enjoying a boom as ten percent more passengers sailed from American ports in 1978 than in 1977.[32] There are many, usually middle- and upper middle-income families, who are faring quite well in spite of inflation. Homeowners have been the biggest winners. Inflation has driven up the price and value of real estate while decreasing the monetary worth of fixed-mortgages.[33]

This discussion has not been intended to minimize the impact of inflation upon upper-income and middle-income families. The effects, particularly the psychological ones, are very real. However, in most discussions of the impact of inflation upon Americans, its victims are usually depicted as the middle-class homeowner struggling to pay a house note and college tuition. Comparatively little mention is given to the impact of inflation on the poor and working-class families. A recent report by the National Advisory Council on Economic Opportunity (NACEO) stated that the combination of inflation and unemployment is forcing many low-income families into debt. This hardship is more glaring, the report maintained, as households in the lowest ten percent income bracket are paying over 119 percent of their net income on food, housing, energy and medical care.[34]

Insecurity, dissatisfaction, discontent and disillusionment are manifestations of the frustrations of the mid-to-late 1970s. These frustrations are being expressed through two types of behavior. One is nostalgia—the longing to return to the good old days. This longing is reflected in the overwhelming popularity of television situation comedies such as "Happy Days" and "Laverne and Shirley;" in the rock and roll revivals featuring stars of the 1950s; the success of the Broadway play and movie "Grease;" and the revival of fashions from earlier decades.[34] The second type of behavior is escapism—an inability to understand fully or to be able to cope with present day realities which has led many people to seek a release. One of the more apparent forms of escapism, both psychologically and physically, has been the disco phenomenon. While dancing has always been a valid art form, disco, with its "fantasties, fashions, gossip and frivolity," expresses narcissism carried to its most hedonistic extreme.[36] Moreover, as numerous observers have noted, disco serves as a convenient escape from social and economic problems,[37] perhaps in the same way that the dance marathons of the 1930s served as releases from the social and economic tensions of the Great Depression.

Is this "meanness mania" part of a recurrent historical pattern or do its antecedents lie in direct response to contemporary social and economic problems? Historians such as Arthur M. Schlesinger, Sr. and Jr., have argued that eras of conservative reaction to liberal reform are part of an "inherent cyclical rhythm in American politics."[38] There is much in the history of the United States during this century to lend strong credence to the cyclical theory of the ebb and flow of liberalism vis-a-vis conservatism.

This conservative reaction, with its undercurrents of meanness and intolerance, has characterized the decades of the 1920s and the 1950s. The 1920s marked both the conservative response to the reforms of the Progressive Era and the national disillusionment with World War I. Arthur M. Schlesinger, Jr. has accurately gauged the nation's mood during the 1920s. He writes:

9

> By 1920, the nation was tired of public crisis. It was tired of discipline and sacrifice. It was tired of abstract and intangible objectives. It could gird itself no longer for heroic moral or intellectual effort. Its instinct for idealism was spent . . . A nation fatigued with ideals and longing for repose was ready for "normalcy." As popular attention receded from public policy, its values and aspirations became private again.[39]

Noted for its "waves of public intolerance seldom felt in the American experience," the decade of the 1920s witnessed the anti-Communist paranoia of the Red Scare, the anti-evolution crusade of religious fundamentalists and the re-emergence of the Ku Klux Klan.[40] Among the factors cited as causes for the decade's increased intolerance were the fear of change, the social tensions arising from economic prosperity and unequal distribution of wealth.[41] These factors are interrelated and help to explain the conservative impulse of the Roaring Twenties. What best captures this impulse is the prevailing fear of further social change, particularly as an explanation for the re-emergence and popularity of the Ku Klux Klan throughout the country. Whereas the Ku Klux Klan had been active in the South, during the 1920s Klan chapters were organized in the Northeast, Midwest and West. In the northern urban centers, the Klan was active among white Protestant Americans who feared the *perceived* threat raised by the increasing black migration to the cities.[42] Many of these very same people were increasingly disturbed by what they perceived as threats to the family and to traditional values. This was particularly evident in the horror with which most Americans viewed the burgeoning feminist movement of the 1920s, and this movement's advocacy of equal rights in employment, pay and birth control.[43] In the same way, the teaching of the theory of evolution in the public schools so unnerved many with fundamentalist beliefs, that the well-known Scopes Case was the result.

These factors—economic discontent amidst prosperity, and fear of social change—coupled with the fear of the spread of Communism, were prevalent during the 1950s. Consequently, the same fear of the continuance of reform, this time a reaction to the New Deal and Fair Deal programs of Franklin D. Roosevelt and Harry S. Truman, reappeared in the 1950s. Perhaps the best and most perceptive analysis of America *circa* 1950 has been offered by historian Eric F. Goldman, a student of American reform movements. Goldman writes:

> No nation can go through such rapid changes in its domestic life without backing up an enormous amount of puzzlement, resentment, and outright opposition. Revolutions provoke counter-revolutions; drastic change, a weariness of change. In this case the reaction was the greater because of the prosperity and enormous social and economic opportunitites which had come to exist by 1949. In social movement, nothing quite fails like too much success. New Dealism having labored mightily to lift low-income Americans

found that it had created a nation of the middle class, shocked at New Dealism's iconoclasm and especially annoyed at its insistence on placing the values of change above those of standard middle-class thinking. Nobody believes more in self-made men than the man who has been made by distant social legislation. No group is more annoyed by reform than those who have benefited from it and no longer need it.[44]

A common theme found both in the Schlesinger and Goldman argument is the American people's weariness of change. Both historians have noted that Americans all too easily retreat from *continued* social change and reform once the most immediate beneficiaries have perceived that further change was neither needed nor desired. Once their needs have been met, then the developing urban middle class of the 1910s or the expanding middle class of the 1930s through 1950s, decide that enough reform has been accomplished.

Just as the 1920s were marked by calls to defend traditional values, so were the 1950s. During the 1950s religious denominations and educational institutions retreated from the ideals and tenets of the social gospel and progressive education, and encouraged conformity and adherence to the status quo. Instead of preaching how to better the lot of individuals, churches preached reassurance and literal interpretations of the Bible.[45] Critics of the American system of public education attacked the progressive education theories of John Dewey. They called for a return to the basics—more discipline in the schools, more work, competition, and the teaching of moral and religious values.[46]

Historians and sociologists have offered numerous interpretations and explanations of the behavior of the American people in the 1950s. Surveying the threat of McCarthyism, they offered explanations of the rise of the "New Conservatism" among liberals in particular, and among the American people in general. Richard Hofstadter, the prominent historian and self-described New Deal liberal, offered an argument in the 1950s that does not differ at all from contemporary neoconservatism. Hofstadter wrote:

> In our day there are some signs that liberals are beginning to find it both natural and expedient to explore the merits and employ the rhetoric of conservatism. They find themselves far more conscious of those things they would like to preserve than they are of those things they would change ... What appeals to me in the New Conservatism is simply the old liberalism, chastened by adversity tempered by time, and by a growing sense of reality.[47]

However, Hofstadter explained the prevalent malaise among Americans as a "Pseudo-conservative revolt." This revolt was fostered by a scramble for status considerations in times of prosperity. During such times, Hofstadter, in trying to explain McCarthyism, contended that status politics were more often expressed in "vindictiveness, in sour memories, in the search for scapegoats, than in realistic proposals for positive action."[48] Following the lead of Hofstadter, sociologists Seymour Martin Lipset, David Riesman and Nathan Glazer explored the roots of discontent in the 1950s. Lipset argued that status-oriented appeals, amidst times of plenty, were popular among those individuals and groups who had risen in economic status, and among those already economically secure who perceived that their status was immediately threatened by lower-status groups.[49] Riesman and Glazer argued that the social discontent was fueled not by the fear of unemployment but by the fear of not knowing what worried them.[50] The Lipset, Riesman and Glazer arguments should be closely examined. When originally offered in the 1950s, these arguments were used as *explanations* of American response to McCarthyism, deemed an aberration from American ideals. When viewed from the vantage point of the 1970s, particularly in light of the present view of both Glazer and Lipset, these arguments can be used, not as explanations of behavior, but as justifications for their present behavior and their present rationale for opposition to programs such as affirmative action and special minority admissions programs.

Having offered an explanation of the historical antecedents and present manifestations of the "meanness mania," this study seeks to explore and counterattack the increasing number of arguments against societal and governmental efforts to ensure equal opportunity in education and in employment for blacks, other minorities and the poor. More specifically, this study is an examination and analysis of specific educational and economic concerns reflective and indicative of the changed mood.

This changed mood manifests itself in the continued attacks on programs deemed both beneficial and useful to blacks. In recent years, social welfare programs, as well as busing and affirmative action programs, have been the subject of much criticism for being "divisive" and "too costly." In a reassessment of these programs and in response to the critics of these programs, this study asserts that social welfare programs, busing and affirmative action are effective strategies to help bring about equal educational and economic opportunities. This study maintains that benefits to blacks and to society as a whole *can* and *do* accrue from both social welfare programs and from voluntary and government-sponsored efforts to bring about increased opportunities for all.

At the same time, the American public school system has come under increasing attack. Critics of the public school system point to how competency based testing and tuition tax credits, and education vouchers will improve the skills of black students and will force public schools to improve through competition. However, this study asserts that these attempts to dismantle or to establish alternatives to the public school system raise more serious threats to the attainment of equal educational opportunity than they offer concrete benefits.

While it is fashionable to criticize *big government* and the American public school system—and many of the criticisms are deserved—much of this criticism purports to reduce big government and to provide alternatives to public education. As the following discussion points out, attacks upon big government, particularly government's role as a provider of social services to those most in need, and attempts to dismantle or to establish alternatives to the public school system pose more serious threats to the attainment of equal opportunity than they offer concrete benefits.

2

The Conservative/
Neo-Conservative
Impulse

Within the past two years, much space and attention have been devoted to the arguments of the growing number of intellectuals and scholars termed neo-conservatives. Much of this writing, particularly that in popular publications and news weeklies, has been attempts to identify individual neo-conservatives and to explain the tenets of neo-conservatism.[1] In addition, neo-conservatives have made repeated use of sympathetic and conservative-minded publications to present and to advance their views. In spite of this increased media exposure, neo-conservatism remains an elusive concept to define. Part of this elusiveness arises from the fact that not all of those who are termed neo-conservatives readily accept the appellation. Some prefer to be described as "neo-liberal" such as Norman Podhoretz and Seymour Martin Lipset; "centrist" such as Midge Decter; and "right wing social democrat" such as Daniel Bell. Only Irving Kristol readily embraces the term.[2] Secondly, there are differences within the ranks of the neo-conservatives. Some, such as Samuel P. Huntington and Edward Banfield, are described as "true-blue neo-conservatives" who are "unabashedly ideological, adamant, hard-hitting, and let the chips fall where they may." The second and larger group, described as "pragmatic neo-conservatives," includes: Irving Kristol, Daniel Bell, Nathan Glazer, Daniel P. Moynihan, James Q. Wilson, Midge Decter, Seymour Martin Lipset, and Ben Wattenberg.[3]

Thus, there is no simple and concise definition of neo-conservatism. A definition/description of neo-conservatism for all practical purposes is "a loose intellectual tendency" composed *principally* but not exclusively of white, male, middle-aged, Jewish intellectuals, formerly of liberal persuasion, who have been tempered by time and by the perceived excesses of the 1960s.[4]

What is presently considered to be neo-conservatism draws its strength from the post World War II "classical liberalism" or "new conservatism." The "classical liberals" or "libertarians" viewed the New Deal welfare state as a serious threat to individual liberty and private enterprise. The "new conservatives" or "traditionalists" sought, in the wake of both fascism and communism, a return to traditional Western religious and ethical values.[5] A reading of the essays and articles of the neo-conservative reveals an adaptation of many of the themes of the classical liberals/new conservatives. Neo-conservatives stress such themes as: stability in the political, social, and economic spheres; values; tradition; liberty; private enterprise; individualism; and firm standards.[6] And, like their forebears, they repeatedly cite Alexis de Tocqueville's *Democracy in America* and Edmund Burke's *Reflections on the Revolution in France,* particularly these writers' fears of the excesses of democracy at the expense of liberty.[7]

What distinguishes the two groups, "new conservatives" and neo-conservatives, is the latter's embrace of the notion of the "conservative welfare state." As envisioned by Kristol, the conservative welfare state would include only those social welfare programs from which all could or would benefit, *i.e.,* Social Security, Medicare, or unemployment compensation.[8] The "classical liberals" have tended to be more doctrinaire in their adherence to free-market principles and abhorence of government social welfare programs. Economist Milton Friedman, considered the dean of the Chicago School of Economics—the practitioners of *laissez-faire* economics—remains most critical of government spending for social welfare programs, particularly Social Security. Former Treasury Secretary William E. Simon bemoans government spending for unemployment compensation, Social Security and government pensions as welfare for the middle and upper classes.[9] Thus, what neo-conservatives see as government-sponsored programs available to all, the new conservatives view as unwise spending.

More recently, there has emerged a younger group of economists of conservative/neo-conservative bent who openly challenge the Keynesian economic theories, the economic basis of the New Deal-Great Society programs. Advocating a lesser role for the government in the economy, these economists apply the technique of cost-benefit analysis to government-sponsored and -financed programs, such as Social Security and unemployment compensation; and, generally conclude that the inflation-increasing costs, outweigh the benefits.[10]

Nevertheless, the 1970s have seen a rapprochement between the "classical liberal-new conservative" and the neo-conservative. This rapprochement, in in-

stances a mutual admiration society, has led to increasing collusion and coopera-
tion between the two groups. Both the American Enterprise Institute for Public
Policy Research (AEI) and the Hoover Institution at Stanford University, once
staunchly conservative think tanks, have attracted several prominent neo-
conservative scholars in the hopes of balancing the scope and thrust of their
research. Thus, with the infusion of neo-conservative thought, these think tanks
have gained increasing acceptability and respectability from academia, the
media and public policymakers.

While the neo-conservatives strongly adhere to many of the beliefs and values
of the new conservatives and the classical liberals, much of their current fame or
notoriety results from their positions on current public policy matters and concerns. At the heart of their arguments is the belief in a more limited role, most
notably in social welfare programs, for local, state and the federal government.
These "limits to social policy," first voiced by Nathan Glazer, are constantly
repeated in the "overload" argument.[11] As the term "overload" is viewed and
used by neo-conservatives, it connotes a government attempt to do too much; one
that is overburdening itself. Thus, to paraphrase the neo-conservative argument,
government should reduce its activities in the social realm. While there are individual differences among the neo-conservatives of when governmental overload
has been reached and how best to reduce it, there is virtual unanimity among
their ranks that governmental programs and regulatory functions should be
reduced and re-ordered.[12] This is the rationale behind much of the neo-
conservative opposition to *big government* and "government intervention and
regulation." Numerous articles attack the concept of government regulation and
the present role of specific government regulatory agencies, particularly those
whose functions entail the protection of minorities, workers, consumers, and the
environment.[13] This argument attacks the "imperial government," in particular
the "imperial judiciary." In recent years, several of the neo-conservatives have
questioned and criticized the increasing role of the federal judiciary in determining public policy. Glazer in particular has criticized the role of federal judges in
ordering mandatory busing and in administering social service programs.[14]

A recurrent fear expressed in much of the writings of neo-conservatives is that
of a "statist" government. As conceptualized by Michael Novak, a statist government is an ever burgeoning and all-encompassing regulatory and welfare state.
To thwart the emergence of a statist government, neo-conservatives call for the
resurrection and resurgence of voluntary associations and institutions; decentralization, if not the virtual elimination of the federal bureaucracy; and respon-
sibilities of the individual.[15]

Many of the neo-conservatives' arguments and concerns, no matter how
neutrally phrased, are often linked to questions of public policy and race. This
linkage continues as neo-conservatives are often quite instrumental in determining, defining, and limiting the thrust of public policy considerations that impact

upon the lives and livelihoods of blacks, other minorities and the poor. Many of their arguments are directed specifically at programs and policies benefiting these groups. Their concerns about governmental "overload" largely address government social welfare programs, particularly those emanating from the Great Society. In the same way, their concerns of imperial government and government regulation pertain to issues largely affecting these groups. Their calls for meritocracy and "rights of the individual" seemed to be used almost exclusively in discussions of affirmative action programs in education and employment.

When neo-conservatives specifically address the status of blacks, they often stress the enormous progress made by blacks over the last twenty-five years. They will cite the economic and social gains of individual blacks as evidence of progress and declining racial discrimination. Such gains, some maintain, will continue as blacks display hard work and individual initiative while relying less and less on governmental assistance.[16] While extolling black progress, some of the neo-conservatives view with contempt the "underclass." This "underclass," by no means all of the urban poor and destitute, is considered to be that group of inner city residents who are poorly educated, unemployed or holding menial jobs. Some neo-conservatives, such as Glazer, express apparent concern with the plight of the "underclass" but are at wits end in coming up with programs and solutions, in place of present strategies, to relieve their plight.[17] Other neo-conservatives take a less sympathetic view and attribute the plight of the underclass to *culture* or to the generosities of "liberal racism." Thus, the failings of the "underclass" are viewed as individual and cultural shortcomings abetted by governmental policies which do not hold them accountable for their actions.[18]

On these issues, neo-conservatism often smacks of an updated application of the nineteenth century survival of the fittest concept. Indeed, several of the arguments of the neo-conservatives, such as Edward Banfield and James Q. Wilson, on crime and poverty, for example, have a strong Spencerian tinge.[19] For these arguments suggest that if an individual is poor, it is due to his or her own failings rather than those of the society. This new devotion to blaming the victim is in direct contradiction to the thrust of the social reform movements of the past four decades. Thus, the neo-conservatives urge policies of inaction based upon their view that some problems, particularly those centered around poverty, are insoluble. They are not prepared to advocate continuing efforts to solve urban ills and reduce social problems. Their advocacy of *lowered expectations* leads to an acceptance of the status quo. But the predicted outcome of governmental inaction bodes far worse for the well-being of society than does continuing the commitment to achieving social and economic justice.

3

The Great Society
Assessed

Conservatives and neo-conservatives continue to attack programs of the Great Society, particularly those designed to benefit blacks and the poor. Former Secretary of the Treasury, William Simon, contends that social programs "roared out of control" during the 1960s, leading to a redistribution of wealth.[1] On the other hand, neo-conservatives continue to attack the "unintended consequences" and *failures* of these programs. While supportive of what he calls a "conservative welfare state," one providing benefits for all groups in society, Irving Kristol still criticizes what he considers to be programs that pit blacks against whites and the poor against the non-poor. Edward Banfield still maintains that the Great Society programs, particularly those in housing, manpower training, and education, were *failures*.[2]

However, newer and more recent critiques and assessments argue, contrary to the assertions of the neo-conservatives, that the Great Society was not a failure, either financially or socially. First, the nation as a whole became aware of the existence of poverty and made a commitment to eradicate poverty. Second, gains have been and are continuing to be realized from the Great Society programs, particularly those in education.

Several recent assessments contend that the Great Society programs, particularly the War on Poverty programs, helped to bring about an awareness in the nation of the extent and nature of poverty and a commitment to reduce it.[3] Positive results, although uneven, have resulted from the War on Poverty. First, both in absolute numbers and in percentages, the number of Americans, black and white, who were considered to be living in poverty declined during

18

the mid to late 1960s. Before the advent of the War on Poverty there were approximately 38 million Americans, 9.9 million blacks and 28.3 million whites, living in poverty. By 1969 that number had decreased to 24.1 million, of whom 7 million were black. As noteworthy as this 25 percent decrease in the number of black Americans living in poverty is, it pales in significance when contrasted with the 43 percent decrease in the number of white Americans living in poverty.[4] Since 1969, however, the forward thrust of the War on Poverty has been retarded by the combination of the Nixon-Ford domestic policies and by two economic recessions, 1969–1971 and 1974–1975, and one predicted recession for late 1979–1980.

Contrary to the arguments of conservative economists such as Martin Anderson and Morton Paglin who contend that the War on Poverty has been won and that the number of poor Americans has been inflated, millions of Americans, black and white, still live in poverty.[5] Such a glaring fact does not, however, support the views of either Kristol or Banfield that the programs of the Great Society were *failures*. Those who have benefited most from the War on Poverty programs, particularly the food stamp program, public assistance, Social Security, and unemployment compensation, have been the residents of rural areas, particularly in the South, and the elderly. The poverty rate for Southern blacks continues to decline, in part from the successes of the civil rights movement and in part from the successes of the Great Society. Since 1969, the poverty rate for Southern blacks has declined 42 percent.[6] Similar gains have been recorded among the elderly. Because of the increase in social security payments and benefits, social security has been described as "the most significant antipoverty measure over the past fifteen years."[7] Its benefits become apparent when one notes that the poverty rate among the elderly has *declined* 41 percent between 1969 and 1976.[8] Thus, social welfare programs, so often criticized, have brought *real* benefits to those in whose behalf they were intended. One such program is the food stamp program, the *bane* of so many conservatives. Yet, the recent findings of a Field Foundation report indicate that food stamps, in reducing malnutrition, "represent one of the unsung yet most effective antipoverty efforts of the last fifteen years."[9]

What becomes apparent is that the continuing commitment to eradicate poverty requires the spending of money, not reductions in social welfare programs. Such a theme is evident in the assessments of those who have studied the funding of the War on Poverty and Great Society programs. Contrary to the arguments of the neo-conservatives, these programs were not overly funded but underfunded. Had they been adequately funded, these programs would have been even more successful.[10] Thus, it was not a case of throwing money at problems, for, in comparison to the funds expended on the war in Vietnam, far fewer funds were spent in implementing the Great Society programs. For example, during fiscal year 1966, $30 billion were spent to finance the war in Vietnam, three times the funds allocated to the Office of Economic Opportunity (OEO) during the years 1965–1970.[11]

Nor is the current level of funding for welfare programs as devastating to the federal budget as some contend. Certainly no friend of the "welfare state", conservative or otherwise, William Simon does argue that spending in behalf of the "genuinely helpless"—Aid for Dependent Children (AFDC) payments and payments to the disabled—has *not* brought about the increased federal budget of the last decade.[12]

In spite of inadequacies in funding and the present hostility directed against them, many of the Great Society programs have been successful and hold promise for future success. However, critics of these programs are quick to trumpet the *failures* or the "unintended consequences" of the programs, but all too conveniently overlook or dismiss the successes. Perhaps the area, aside from the three major pieces of civil rights legislation (The Civil Rights Act of 1964, the Voting Rights Act of 1965 and the Fair Housing Act of 1968), in which the Great Society programs has enjoyed the most success, has been in education. From the Head Start program through increased federal support for undergraduate and graduate education, blacks and other minorities have benefited from programs designed to maximize increased equal educational opportunity.

Recent empirical data are appearing that refute earlier research criticizing these programs. Early studies, such as the 1969 Westinghouse Report, indicated minimal and often short-lived gains for children who had been enrolled in Head Start.[13] However, subsequent research is more encouraging. A review of ninety-six studies of Head Start programs has indicated that these programs are successful in reducing school failure, raising IQ scores, improving reading scores, and in helping children to develop and maintain self-confidence. More importantly, these gains were not temporary, as skills that had been developed in Head Start helped students several years after their participation in the program.[14] The results of one of these programs, described as "typical," are quite impressive. In the Nashville, Tennessee Head Start program it was found:

> At the end of third grade, 92 percent of the program children were receiving passing grades while only 60 percent of control children were. Twenty-six percent of program children were at or above their expected grade level, compared with 8 percent for the control group. Only 3 percent of the program children had fallen more than a year and a half below grade level, compared with 32 percent of control children. Children in the program were consistently superior to children in the control group in grades in reading, arithmetic and language, more than half the program children scored at or above their expected level, less than 20 percent of the control group did so.[15]

20

Nor is Head Start a static bureaucracy, one not seeking to improve or upgrade programs. For, if further improvements in Head Start programs are to continue, modifications and innovations, such as funding exemplary programs to serve as pilots, must continue.[16]

Studies also indicate that compensatory programs in the early years can bring about impressive results. While critics of compensatory education point out some of the shortcomings and inadequacies of the Follow Through program, a federal program designed to measure the gains of Head Start programs, they fail to mention the successful programs and what can be learned from them.[17] Yet, children in New York City who had enrolled in Follow Through were found to be reading *significantly better* than would be expected from their earlier scores. It was also reported that children who were enrolled in Follow Through for the full four years, from kindergarten through third grade, scored *significantly better* on tests than those who were registered in the program for a shorter period or not registered at all.[18]

Perhaps equally as successful as the Head Start and Follow Through programs is Title I of the Elementary and Secondary Education Act of 1965. Studies of the effectiveness of Title I programs point to a positive impact. Analyses of state and school district reports have found increased educational and achievement gains for children enrolled. Based upon their review of Title I programs, Sar A. Levitan and Robert Taggart conclude:

> (t)here is no doubt, however, that compensatory education programs have the potential to significantly raise the learning rates of the disadvantaged as they have done in some areas. The positive evidence is also more recent, probably reflecting real improvement in design and administration.[19]

Just as impressive, if not more so, has been the dramatic increase in college attendance among blacks, particularly between 1964 and the present. This increase coincided with the passage of both civil rights and higher education legislation and an increase in the activism of black students.[20] The Civil Rights Act of 1964 called for the desegregation of dual racial systems of public and non-profit educational institutions and prohibited racial discrimination in federally assisted programs. Such legislation has helped to increase both the number and the percentage of colleges and universities enrolling black students. In the same way, the Upward Bound program, designed to provide both remedial help and counseling to low income high school students interested in attending college, has helped to increase college attendance among blacks. Nearly all students attending Upward Bound programs graduate from high school, with two-thirds of the enrollees going on to attend college.[21]

Equally important to the advances made by blacks in higher education has been Title III of the Higher Education Act of 1965 and the Higher Education Act Amendments of 1972. Title III, designed to strengthen "developing institutions," has benefited black colleges and universities, albeit in an uneven pattern, as there is a declining amount of funds being allocated for traditionally black institutions. On the whole, from fiscal years 1966 through 1977, black institutions received an average of 53.08 percent of the $471 million allocated, a combined sum of just over 250 million dollars. The Higher Education Act of 1972 provides financial assistance: Basic Educational Opportunity Grants (BEOGs), Supplemental Educational Opportunity Grants (SEOGs), and the College Work Study Program. Based upon 1976-1977 data, black students received "a relatively high percentage of Federal funds."[22] Roughly 11 percent of those enrolled in colleges and universities during academic year 1976-1977, black students received 29.6 percent of the BEOG's awarded that year.[23]

What becomes clear is that black students and institutions have profited from these programs. Just as apparent is the need to continue, if not to expand, the scope and funding for these programs. While the funding for Head Start programs has increased nearly eight-fold, from $83 million to $680 million over the last fourteen years, a majority of children eligible for participation in Head Start programs still do not have the opportunity because of inadequate funds.[24] Because of inadequate funding, not as many children as are eligible take advantage of Title I programs. It has been estimated that in New York City alone, there are 151,000 pupils who are eligible for Title I programs but who do not participate.[25] Positive steps, however, have been taken by the Carter administration to increase funding for both Head Start and Title I.

Admittedly, compensatory education programs are not flawless, but their shortcomings in administration and implementation can be corrected. The major shortcomings are inadequate funding and continuous changes in the programs. However, even Paul Copperman, a severe critic of the implementation and administration of these programs, does not call for their abolition.[26] Thus, the bottom line in assessing these programs is not the impracticality of "throwing money at problems" but that "money can make a difference."[27]

Assessments of the much-maligned manpower training programs do show economic and social gains accruing to those taking part in such programs. Economist Andrew Brimmer maintains that programs under the Manpower Development and Training Act have been "worthwhile" and beneficial to blacks and whites.[28] Likewise, the Job Corps, so often criticized, is now described as one of "the more successful efforts to come out of President Johnson's War on Poverty."[29] A 1975 assessment of the Job Corps points to the educational and vocational gains made by enrollees. Often lacking in educational skills, they have made considerable gains in both reading and arithmetic. More important, however, have been the gains made by those enrollees who remained in the program. Such persons have done considerably better in the job market, experiencing lower unemployment and enjoying higher wages.[30] Equally significant has been the Job Corps' success in teaching and instilling desirable work and social habits. The analysis concludes:

> Taken as a whole, the assessments of the program give a clearly positive reading. Almost all studies have found that corpsmen are better off after the program than they were on entrance, whether this standard of measurement is employment, earnings, educational level, motivation, or work habits. The longer the stay, the greater the beneficial impacts seem to be. Whether these benefits outweigh the high cost per person. It seems indisputable that at least for some of these hard-core disadvantaged youths, the Job Corps succeeded where other educational and vocational efforts had failed.[31]

Thus, such programs designed to train or retrain workers so that they may be able to find jobs or escape low-paying ones, were and are well worth the costs involved. Facing an option of training and retraining workers or paying unemployment and welfare benefits, it is clear that the country as a whole stands to gain *more* from increasing the number of employable persons than the number of "unemployables."

While there have been shortcomings and limitations inherent in some of the manpower programs, especially in fraud and human error, such problems do not and should not detract from the legitimacy and soundness of government training programs to stem unemployment. The need for the continuation and maintenance of programs such as Comprehensive Employment and Training Act (CETA) become all the more apparent when one realizes the lack of total commitment by the private sector in providing training and employment. Moreover, it is too early to write off such job training programs as *failures*. More than likely, there are possible ripple effects from such programs. Black participation and involvement in the various jobs programs offered invaluable leadership and entrepreneural opportunities, the benefits from which may be apparent only in future years.[32]

An assessment of Great Society programs, contrary to the cost-benefit analyses of their critics, shows more successes than failures. Conservative and neo-conservative critics continually stress alleged costs of social welfare programs, but their inherent biases prevent them from applying their techniques to the far more costly and inefficient military expenditures. Moreover, as Henry J. Aaron points out in *Politics and the Professors: The Great Society in Perspective*, public mood and political philosophy are dictated by and reflective of the nature of research and evaluation. Thus, in an era when government is viewed with suspicion and hostility, this skeptical mood is compounded by the "profoundly conservative tendency" of research and evaluation.[33] But a cost-benefit analysis based upon gains to society counters this conservative tendency noted by Aaron. Government spending for social welfare programs, designed to uplift and improve the lives and livelihoods of blacks and the poor, is certainly more beneficial to society than allowing the continued existence of poverty, with its potentially disruptive effects upon society. Certainly, spending for manpower programs, which produces employable workers, is far more cost-efficient and beneficial than providing continued welfare payments. Government spending for educational and educational-support programs allows individuals to realize their potential and helps to maximize equal opportunity.

How then does one realistically evaluate the Great Society? Perhaps the comments of Sar A. Levitan and Robert Taggart best express the accomplishments of Lyndon Johnson's administration. Fully conscious of both the successes and the shortcomings, they conclude:

> The Great Society did not eliminate poverty, but the number of poor was reduced and their deprivation significantly alleviated. The Great Society did not equalize the status of blacks and other minorities, but substantial gains were made which have not been completely eroded. Significant redistribution of income was not achieved or sought, but the disadvantaged and disenfranchised were helped. The Great Society did not have any magic formula for prosperity but its policies contributed to the longest period of sustained growth in the nation's history. It did not revamp education, or assure health care for everyone, or feed all the hungry, but as a result of its efforts, the disadvantaged were considerably better educated, fed, and cared for.[34]

4

Black Progress: Myths and Realities

The social, economic and political gains made by blacks over the twenty-five years since the *Brown* decision are the direct results of the successes of the civil rights movement. Overt racial barriers in education, employment and housing have been removed by court decisions and the passage of state and federal laws. Unfortunately, the gains made by blacks, individually and collectively, have blinded too many Americans to the grim reality: the masses of black Americans have yet to experience equal opportunity in education, employment and housing.

A recurrent finding in several public opinion polls conducted during the years 1977 through 1979 is that white Americans believe that black Americans have made great progress toward achieving equality and that blacks are no longer the victims of discrimination. Further, progress by blacks, they believe, should not come through government assistance but through the efforts of blacks themselves.[1]

Blacks are mindful of the *degree* of progress achieved thus far; however, the black perception of his or her status is hardly as optimistic as that of whites. Blacks remain unconvinced that the elimination of racial discrimination is now a *fait accompli*. According to a 1977 Lou Harris poll, a majority of blacks stated that discrimination still existed in job opportunities, skilled and unskilled; pay; housing; quality public education; union membership; and treatment by police and protection against crime.[2] The most recent Harris poll on racial attitudes has found less optimism in 1978 among blacks than in an earlier poll. On the issues of employment, job advancement, equal pay, and decent housing, the percentage of black respondents who indicated that blacks were discriminated against in

25

these areas rose.[3] Interpreting the differences in black-white perceptions of racial progress, Harris notes:

> There is little doubt that most blacks in 1978 still feel their status is very much at a second-class level. By the same token, whites see much of the former discrimination now so alleviated that it is well on the way to being wiped out. The two groups—black and white—may feel they are observing the phenomenon, the status of discrimination against blacks. But, in the case of blacks, they are talking about the daily consequences in their own lives of less than equal treatment, while whites are dealing with their own behavior and that of the society they dominate in how it does or does not give blacks a fair chance. For blacks, the pain of discrimination can be highly personal and costly. For whites, their major source of pain in this process can be a guilty conscience. In this uneven process, felt discrimination can be consuming. For whites, the way to ease a potentially gnawing conscience is to see the progress, rationalizing how much worse things could have been for blacks had the past 15 years not been lived through.[4]

What, aside from guilt, reinforces these perceptions of black progress by whites? For one, numerous lay and scholarly articles depict the economic progress of the new black middle class or the emergent *black elite*. These accounts note the increased numbers of black youths in institutions of higher education, the increased numbers of black families earning in excess of $15,000 yearly, the inroads of blacks into better paying jobs and professions.[5] Nathan Glazer's overly optimistic assessment reflects the tone of this commentary. He writes:

> . . . integration in general has made enormous advances since 1954. It has been advanced by the hundreds of thousands of blacks in Northern and Southern colleges. It has been advanced by the hundreds of thousands of blacks who have moved into professional and white-collar jobs in government, in the universities, in the school systems, in business. It has been advanced by the steady rise in black income which offers many blacks the opportunity to live in integrated areas. Most significantly, it has been advanced because millions of blacks now vote—in the South as well as the North—and because hundreds of blacks have been elected to school committees, city councils, state legislatures, the Congress. This is what is creating an integrated society in the United States.[6]

Such political, economic and social gains *should* be noted, applauded and encouraged as positive indicators of how the efforts by blacks, coupled with government intervention via legislation and affirmative action regulations, can increase opportunities for blacks. However, one cannot or should not view this progress apart from the grim reality of life for the majority of blacks who have yet to experience equal opportunity in education, employment and housing. Nor should the constantly expressed concern by black leaders and spokespersons about the economic and social plight of the black masses be interpreted as ''failure-mongering'' or the disavowing of black progress.[7] For, at best, the progress made by blacks has been *uneven* and *inconsistent,* determined to a great extent by the state of the economy. Aside from these two qualifiers, the progress of blacks has been *relative,* both in terms of the numbers of blacks who are benefiting and in comparison to the progress made by whites.

Figure 1 shows the sizeable increase in the number of black students attending college since 1970. However, it does not show what types of institutions black students are attending, nor does it compare in absolute numbers this phenomenal surge. Several ISEP publications illustrate quite clearly that this increased participation over the past few years has been largely at the two year college level.[8] According to enrollment figures for academic year 1976-77, 50 percent of the black undergraduate students were enrolled in two year colleges.[9] Besides having uneven distribution in institutions of higher education, blacks have not obtained parity, in terms of the relevant age group population, in undergraduate age group population, and in undergraduate enrollment. Because of the still high attrition rates of black high school students, there remains a "disproportionate limitation on college attendance among blacks."[10]

Again, the increase in earnings of individual black families must be carefully weighed against both the continuing high rates of unemployment of black males, females and teenagers and the declining median income for blacks. Figure 2 shows the continuing high rate of black unemployment over the past decade compared to that of whites.

FIGURE 1

Selected Examples of Black Economic and Social Progress, 1970-1977

UPWARD-BOUND BLACKS

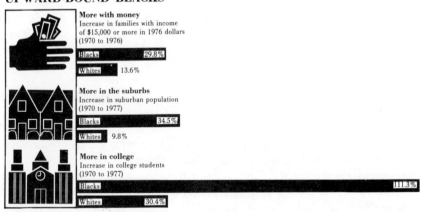

More with money
Increase in families with income of $15,000 or more in 1976 dollars (1970 to 1976)

Blacks 29.8%
Whites 13.6%

More in the suburbs
Increase in suburban population (1970 to 1977)

Blacks 34.5%
Whites 9.8%

More in college
Increase in college students (1970 to 1977)

Blacks 111.3%
Whites 30.4%

SOURCE: *U.S. News and World Report,* 5 June 1978, p. 51.

27

FIGURE 2

Black and White Unemployment, 1967-1978

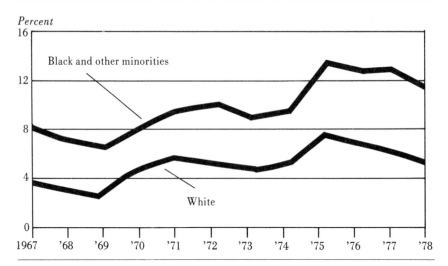

SOURCE: Bureau of Labor Statistics from *Chicago Tribune*, 21 January 1979, Sec. 3, p. 4.

As can be seen, the unemployment rate for blacks has generally been double that of whites. In 1975, the overall black unemployment rate was 1.8 times higher than the white unemployment rate. In 1978 the unemployment rate of blacks was 2.3 times higher than that of whites.[11] According to the National Urban League, this differential is "the widest it has ever been since the Unites States Department of Labor began recording job statistics by race."[12] The most recent data from the Bureau of Labor Statistics indicate no lessening of the gap. In June 1979, the unemployment rate for black adult males (7.9 percent) was 2.3 times that of white adult males (3.4 percent). The rate for black females (10.8 percent) was 2.1 times that of white females. (5 percent). The rate for black teenagers (34 percent) was 2.6 times that of white teenagers (13 percent).[13]

The concern expressed over unemployment is much higher among blacks than it is among whites. According to one Chicago poll, two-thirds of the blacks polled cited unemployment as their number one worry, ahead of crime and inflation.[14] Yet, as bad a problem as blacks perceive unemployment to be, conservative and neo-conservative scholars and economists have argued that employment is not all that serious. On the one hand, they argue that current unemployment figures, including figures for women and teenagers, are inflated when compared to past figures which included only male heads of households. At the same time, some argue, as does Martin Feldstein, that unemployment insurance deters many from

28

actively seeking employment.[15] These critics maintain that unemployment insurance, often paying more than the minimum wage, deters people from seeking work. With increased unemployment among women, black women in particular, and the rising number of single-parent households, what is the alternative for many of these women but to seek public assistance, the bane of conservatives? Moreover, unemployment insurance is not necessarily the good life that critics depict. The benefits from unemployment insurance have often been overestimated and cannot compensate either for the loss of self-esteem or the ability to satisfactorily rejoin the labor market.[16]

When these scholars do assess the impact of high unemployment rates, they usually focus on black teenagers. Scholars such as Thomas Sowell, Walter Williams and Finis Welch attribute the high unemployment rate among black teenagers to "government restrictions," particularly the minimum wage.[17] But racial discrimination in the market place is still a significant factor, as minimum wage legislation does not have the same disproportionate impact upon white teenagers as it does upon blacks. The unemployment rate for black youths who have attended college (27.2 percent) or graduated from high school (23.6 percent) is *higher* than the unemployment rate for white high school dropouts (22.3 percent).[18] It is obvious that black teenagers are still outside the informal network of friends and relatives that alerts white youths to the availability of jobs. The workings of this network are quite apparent in the ease with which the children of members of Congress and high ranking government officials have been able to obtain summer jobs, while inner-city black youths have far more problems and far fewer successes.[19] Thus, arguments based on *culture, values,* and *traditions* cannot fully explain the inability of black youths to find employment.

Contrary to the Glazer argument cited earlier, the median income of black families as compared to white families is no longer increasing but decreasing. The present figure is 57.1 percent, the lowest percentage in a dozen years. This decreasing percentage is largely attributable to the fact that the real median income for blacks has not improved over the last three years, while that for whites has improved.[20] Figure 3 illustrates the rise and fall of black family median income as a percentage of white income.

Yet, those like Thomas Sowell who oversell black progress would attribute the decline in black median income to the "failures" of affirmative action. At the same time, they proclaim the parity in income achieved by a small number of blacks.[21] But this income parity is confined to a select subgroup of blacks—recent college graduates.[22] Richard B. Freeman's recent work, *Black Elite: The New Market for Highly Qualified Blacks,* rightly attributes much of this income parity to the characteristics of individual blacks as well as to affirmative action programs and increased government hiring of blacks.[23] But, perhaps Freeman slightly overexaggerates the market for black college graduates. Reports from placement agencies, catering almost exclusively to placing black college

FIGURE 3

Black Income as a Percentage of White Income, 1965-1978

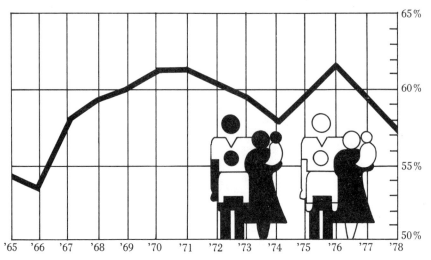

Median family income based on Census Bureau surveys taken in March of each year.

SOURCE: *Wall Street Journal*, 6 March 1979, p. 48.

graduates, are not quite as optimistic as Freeman. In spite of stepped-up corporate recruiting, there is still a problem of underemployment for minority college graduates with technical and professional degrees.[24] Moreover, according to
reports from black colleges, recent graduates are receiving salary offers close to
the national average and in some cases slightly below the national average. Such
findings, according to Richard Clark Associates, strongly contradict the stories of
recent black college graduates receiving extremely high starting salaries.[25]

Furthermore, a closer examination of the economic gains of black middle-
income and upper-income families reveals no real increase. Based upon 1977
data, only one-fourth of black families had annual incomes exceeding the U.S.
Bureau of Labor Statistics figure of $17,106, the intermediate standard of living
for an American family. This proportion was the same as 1973. Although the
percentage for white families dropped by one percentage point overall from 1973
to 1977, from 50 percent to 49 percent, the proportion of white families enjoying
middle-income status still exceeded the proportion of blacks by a two-to-one
margin.[26] For higher income families, black and white, the disparity is even
greater. Only nine percent of black families had incomes over $25,202, the
budget level for "higher standard of living". This figure is a three percent drop
from the percentage of black upper-income families in 1972. On the other hand,

the proportion of white families whose income surpassed the Bureau of Labor Statistics (BLS) figure increased from 23 percent to 24 percent.[27] Thus, it is clear that these economic gains can be short-lived, subject to downward changes in the economy. In assessing the uncertain economic status of the black middle class, particularly in a worsening economy, Vernon Jordan has stated, "most of us will have to take off these Brooks Brothers suits".[28]

Race vs Class: How Significant the Decline?

Adding to the glaring misperception of the degree of black progress has been the recent publication of a highly controversial book, *The Declining Significance of Race* by University of Chicago sociologist William Julius Wilson. Wilson argues that at the present time class has more to do in determining the life chances of individual blacks in the economic sphere than does race. As a result of the success of the civil rights movement and government legislation in eliminating most overt forms of discrimination, Wilson argues, "talented and educated" blacks can move into prestigious jobs, in both the public and private sectors. Although there has been a "remarkable shift in the black occupational structure," government policies and changes in the economy have "not benefitted the black underclass." Their lives and livelihoods, he notes, are marred by unemployment, declining participation in the labor market, increased welfare dependence and poverty. Consequently, Wilson asserts, there are growing class divisions emerging among blacks.[29] More recently, Wilson has addressed these alleged divisions. He notes a class vote among blacks on Proposition 13—blacks who owned property voted for Proposition 13, while blacks who rented voted against Proposition 13. Moreover, "articulate" and "elite" blacks paid more attention to the *Bakke* case than to the Humphrey-Hawkins bill.[30]

The Wilson thesis is not without assumptions that are subject to debate. The two most telling points of contention are 1) the degree to which race has declined as a factor, and 2) the degree and extent of class division among blacks. Critics of the Wilson thesis, most notably sociologist Kenneth Clark and educator Charles V. Willie, argue that Wilson underestimates severely the continuing role of race. Arguing that "race is still the dominant factor in determining blacks' chances in life," Clark contends that the number of blacks in government and corporate positions of privilege and power is "miniscule."[31] Like Clark, Willie contends that race is still a barrier to economic opportunity and advancement, especially for middle class blacks. According to Willie the difference in income between black and white professionals is greater than the difference in income between blacks and whites holding nonprofessional jobs.[32]

A 1977 report by the Equal Employment Opportunity Commission (EEOC), and a recent survey published in the *National Law Journal* lend strong support to the critics of the Wilson thesis. Entitled "Black Experiences vs. Black Expectations," the EEOC study points out that in the period 1969 through 1974, the percentage of blacks in managerial and official positions rose from 1.4 to 2 percent. At the same time the number of black professionals and technicians rose by one percent. According to the report, "Black professional employment in professional jobs has almost stabilized since the employment gap did not materially change between 1969 and 1974."[33]

The current situation of black lawyers mirrors that of other black professionals. While the overall number of black lawyers has increased in recent years, blacks comprise only 2 percent of the legal profession, 11,000 out of 525,000. But of the estimated 3,700 partners in the fifty largest American law firms only twelve, or 3 percent, are black. These results indicate quite clearly that "blacks have made few inroads at major firms."[34] When asked about these stark disparities, several black lawyers cite their lack of contacts among potential clients; *i.e.*, they do not have the same or equivalent access to privilege and power as white lawyers. They also cite the firms' lack of sincere commitment in recruiting blacks, racism in the awarding of the more lucrative and rewarding cases, and a lack of success in breaking into the "old boy network."[35]

Likewise, the current situation of black and minority journalists indicates the difficulties of gaining access to privilege and power. While the number of minority journalists has quadrupled over the last decade, minorities make up only four percent of the profession. Moreover, two-thirds of the nation's daily newspapers still do not have even one minority professional.[36] Table 1 illustrates the progress and lack of progress in hiring by many of the major dailies.

While Wilson tends to overstate the role of class as a factor, he does recognize the plight of the poor and advocates governmental policies—such as a full employment program—that seek to relieve the problem.[37] However, conservative and neo-conservative supporters of Wilson's thesis have so misconstrued this idea of class as to suggest that race-conscious remedies such as affirmative action programs in employment and special minority admissions are unnecessary. In liner notes for *The Declining Significance of Race,* Glazer has written:

> Wilson's analysis of the problem of the black lower class is one of the best I've seen. It is a good and valuable work in defining just where the problem is—and where it isn't.[38]

While Glazer professes sympathy for the lower class, his questioning of further government efforts in behalf of blacks and the poor belies his apparent concern. Both Sowell and Williams make use of the Wilson thesis to advance their own arguments. According to Sowell, poor job skills and school work, *i.e.*, "class characteristics," are more harmful to black advancement than race.[39] Williams maintains that "privileged blacks," himself excluded, often support policies such as minimum wage legislation that restrict the "underclass."[40] Yet Williams

TABLE 1

The Minority Presence on Selected Newspaper Staffs

Newspaper or Chain	Number of Journalists	Minority Journalists	Percent Minority
Albuquerque Journal	70	3	4.3%
Akron Beacon Journal	106	12	11.3
Arizona Star	75	9	12.0
Atlanta Constitution	110	9	8.2
Atlanta Journal	156	5	3.2
Arkansas Gazette	80	2	2.5
Austin American Statesman	100	7	7.0
Baltimore News American	110	16	14.5
Boston Globe	330	16	4.8
Charlotte News	69	5	7.2
Charlotte Observer	120	7	5.8
Chicago Sun Times	266	28	10.5
Chicago Tribune	430	19	4.4
Corpus Christi Caller and Times	80	8	10.0
Dayton Daily News	80	8	10.0
Dayton Journal Herald	65	8	12.3
Des Moines Register and Tribune	199	10	5.0
Detroit Free Press	155	10	6.4
El Paso Herald-Post	32	5	15.6
El Paso Times	65	23	35.4
Gannett Newspapers	2715	147	5.4
Harte-Hanks Southwest Group	90	3	3.3
Houston Post	125	6	4.8
Jackson Daily News	40	3	7.5
Knight-Ridder Newspapers*	4762	287	6.0
Linsay-Schaub Newspapers	234	4	1.7
Los Angeles Herald-Examiner	135	12	8.9
Los Angeles Times	572	28	4.9
Memphis Commercial Appeal	120	5	4.2
Miami Herald**	320	51	15.9
Miami News	75	4	5.3
Minneapolis Tribune	135	5	3.7
Minneapolis Star	119	4	3.4
Newsday	319	18	5.6
New York Times	670	40	6.0
Oakland Press (Michigan)	63	9	14.3
Ottaway Newspapers	492	5	1.0
Palm Beach Times and Post	125	5	4.0
Philadelphia Bulletin	274	14	5.1
Philadelphia Inquirer	250	17	6.8
Port Arthur News	36	3	8.3
Portland Oregonian	167	4	2.4

Newspaper or Chain	Number of Journalists	Minority Journalists	Percent Minority
Raleigh News & Observer	75	3	4.0
Rochester Democrat & Chronicle and Times-Union	216	11	5.1
St. Louis Post Dispatch	180	20	11.1
San Angelo Times (Texas)	52	4	7.6
San Diego Union	140	7	5.0
San Francisco Examiner	200	23	11.5
Springfield Union and Daily News (Massachusetts)	160	2	1.2
Springfield Sun and News (Ohio)	40	1	2.5
Trenton Times	93	4	4.3
Tucson Daily Citizen	75	3	4.0
United Press International	857	52	6.0
Waco Tribune-Herald	50	1	2.0
Wall Street Journal	220	12	5.4
Washington Post	353	35	9.9
Washington Star	186	10	5.4

SOURCE: Nick Kotz, "The Minority Struggle for a Place in the Newsroom." *Columbia Journalism Review,* 17 (March/April 1979):26.

NOTE: These statistics cover professional news employees—editors copy desk personnel, reporters, and photographers—at 186 daily newspapers and United Press International. (The Associated Press declined to make figures available.) They are based on interviews with newspaper-group executives, newspaper editors, and reporters conducted by the author, with the assistance of Jim Dawson.

*Includes some managerial and professional personnel outside the news departments.

**Includes 30 Hispanic employees of a special Spanish-language section.

and Sowell, both advocates of *laissez-faire* economic policies, would not back any legislation calling for government as the employer of last resort.

Are class differences between the black middle class and the "underclass" as divisive as Wilson and others contend? And is black leadership as out of touch as Sowell would suggest? Many of the very persons that Wilson labels "articulate" and "elite" blacks, were among those who criticized the passage of Proposition 13 as an attempt to reduce social services, particularly services used primarily by blacks, other minorities and the poor. While many of this same elite opposed the suits alleging reverse discrimination filed by Allen Bakke and Brian Weber, their attention and efforts were neither distracted from nor led to the weakening of the Humphrey-Hawkins bill. Black organizations and civil rights groups lobbied strenuously in support of the Humphrey-Hawkins bill. One cannot attribute elitist tendencies to members of the Congressional Black Caucus, certainly not Representative John Conyers, who urged President Carter to take a more active role in trying to prevent the watering-down of the bill. The elite whom Wilson should be addressing are not his critics, but supporters of his thesis. For it is they who are the most critical of government efforts in behalf of blacks, other minorities and the poor.

Moreover, is there an estrangement between the black middle class and the black lower class as depicted by some impressionistic writing?[41] More concrete evidence suggests that this schism is not as real as suggested. A recent study of 178 middle class black families by Dr. Harriette McAdoo reveals that those blacks with middle-income salaries and lifestyles are not personally detached from their relatives and friends. She contends that the black kinship network based upon mutual aid and support still remains viable, not out of obligation but more out of a sense of "this is what is done in families."[42] This same concern is manifested in the support of black civil rights, professional and social organizations for activities to benefit lower-income groups and blacks as a group.

Studies of the political behavior of members of the black middle class indicate that they do not differ significantly from that of lower-income blacks. Charles Hamilton, in a study of the voting behavior of blacks, Jews and Italians in New York City on bonds, propositions, and amendments, found that on nearly all issues there was more agreement among black middle-class and lower-class voters than among the other groups.[43] In interpreting his data Hamilton asserts:

> ... my research to date does not show that black middle-class voters tend to be more conservative than black lower-class voters—or tend to behave more like their white middle-class counterparts. In fact, just the opposite. The black middle-class voters tend to be more liberal in their electoral choices than all the other class and ethnic groupings.[44]

Alan Monroe's study, *Public Opinion in America,* reaches the same conclusion about black attitudes on economic issues. He argues that blacks tend to be the "most liberal of the major demographic groupings" on economic issues. And, he maintains, middle-class blacks are just as "liberal" as lower-class blacks.[45] Assessing black liberalism on these issues, Monroe notes:

> most blacks are poor, naturally leading to economic liberalism, and it may be that middle-class blacks continue to identify with the problems and aspirations of the rest of the black community to a greater extent than upwardly mobile whites do with the community they leave behind. Another factor is that blacks have more reason to be more enthusiastic about the efficacy of governmental action particularly at the federal level, for it is in the public arena that some of their gains have come.[46]

The alleged schism between the black middle class and lower class is more apparent than real. On political and economic issues, there are only minimal differences among blacks. Both classes support governmental actions, contrary to the arguments of black conservatives, and both recognize the continuing role of race in political and economic spheres.

35

5

Attacks on American Public Education

Is there, as a 1979 editorial in the *New York Times* proclaimed, "an open season on public schools".[1] The increased printed and vocal attacks directed against public school education and higher education lead one to believe that the American system of education is the victim of this open season. Judging from the nature of these attacks and the ideological diversity of the attackers, fewer and fewer Americans are pleased with schools and the current state of education within the nation.

Historically, controversies surrounding the nature of American public and higher education and the role of the school system have continually been debated among educational reformers and more conservative-minded individuals and institutions. Central to these debates, and consequently central to the thrust of the movements for education reform, were such questions as: who was and who was not to benefit from access to public education, how and for what reasons were individuals to benefit, what curriculum was to be taught and how was it to be taught.[2]

Within the past decade attacks against the educational establishment have been launched by more radical critics, some of whom question the ability of schools to make a difference in pupils' lives. Yet, a far larger number of critics contend that schools are not doing a very good job in educating students. Over the past six years the Gallup Poll has noted decreased public confidence in the public schools.[3] Among the factors cited as causes for this decreasing confidence were: lack of discipline; drug use; lack of proper financial support; school desegregation and busing; inadequate curricula and low standards; difficulty in hiring and maintaining good teachers; classroom size; lack of student interest; crime and vandalism; and lack of parental interest.[4]

More radical critics question the effectiveness of education reform, particularly within the present confines of American society. In *Inequality*, Christopher Jencks and associates contend that increased expenditures for compensatory education programs do not necessarily result in higher test scores. Instead, they advocate a redistribution of income which would "break the link between vocational success and living standards."[5] Samuel Bowles and Herbert Gintis, in *Schooling in Capitalist America*, argue that educational reform movements by and large have been unsuccessful inasmuch as they do not question the basic economic ordering of American society.[6]

Anthropologist John U. Ogbu, in *Minority Education and Caste* offers an assessment similar to that of Bowles and Gintis. He contends that the American caste system, by channeling black adults into menial and inferior jobs, has conditioned black children not to do well in school. To relieve and reverse this systematic trend, Ogbu argues that "equality of post-school opportunity"—the elimination of caste barriers—will have to be achieved. Once the barriers have been eliminated, Ogbu asserts, blacks' attitudes toward schools and schooling will change.[7] A very recent study by Richard DeLone, entitled *Small Futures: Children, Inequality and the Limits of Liberal Reform*, combines the theses of Jencks and associates, Bowles and Gintis and Ogbu in assessing what determines success in this country. DeLone maintains that unemployment and the unequal distribution of income severely limit the degree of social and economic mobility.[8]

A common theme in all of these books is criticism of the limitations of social reform. Such statements could be used by policymakers to curtail or to eliminate many social welfare programs inasmuch as some analysts have argued that these policies are ineffective. As the earlier discussion of the Great Society programs has pointed out, efforts at early childhood education, such as Head Start, have been relatively successful. Both Ogbu and DeLone, in spite of their criticisms of the nature of reform within the present context of American society, recognize the benefits of reform. Ogbu contends that social welfare programs are necessary, but that they are only a partial remedy. DeLone defends social welfare efforts, arguing that "simply eliminating those systems would be irresponsible."[9] More radical critics of the American public school system point to shortcomings in society as reasons why educational reforms have not been as successful as hoped. However, these critics, especially Ogbu and DeLone, recognized that the maintenance and continuance of social welfare programs are steps, albeit partial, toward the attainment of equality and equity in the larger society.

The second, and broader-based group of critics are the parents, educators, and employers who argue that public schools are not doing a good job in educating students. Repeatedly, they have voiced cries of "grade inflation," "social promotion," and "functional illiteracy." And, like the 1950s critics of progressive education, many of them are voicing opposition to educational innovations. These critics attack such programs as open classrooms, more relevant curricula and alternative modes of instruction. In their place, they support a "back-to-basics" movement, stressing the teaching of basic skills in reading, writing and mathematics. They also stress a return to firm standards in grading, more structured modes of instruction and more homework.

Reflective of this mood are two recent books, Christopher Lasch's *The Culture of Narcissism: American Life in an Age of Diminishing Expectations* and Paul Copperman's *The Literacy Hoax: The Decline of Reading, Writing, and Learning in the Public Schools, and What We Can Do About It.* As can be ascertained by their titles, these works are rather harsh assessments of American public education. Lasch argues that the attempt to spread mass education "has contributed to the decline of critical thought and the erosion of intellectual standards." This deterioration, he laments, has led to the "spread of stupidity" in the country.[10] In equally shrill and bitter language, Copperman bemoans a "literacy hoax," a spreading decline of reading, writing and learning among students from all social and economic groups.[11] Both authors call for a return to teaching basic skills and upholding firm standards.

The growing competency based testing movement, to be discussed later, is perhaps the present focal point of the back-to-basics movement. To date, over thirty state systems of education have implemented competency based testing as a means of curbing "social promotion" and "functional illiteracy." However, as shown by the results from states who have implemented the requirement that students pass an "exit exam" before they receive a high school diploma, competency based testing poses a serious threat to black attainment of equal educational opportunity.

This is not to suggest that the back-to-basics movement is overtly detrimental to blacks. The shortcomings of competency based testing lie in how it is implemented, rather than in its alleged aims. Moreover, black parents and educators, who have long noted the shortcomings of the public school system in educating black children, have always been among those calling for a return to the teaching of basic skills, better discipline in the schools and an end to "social promotions."[12]

While the back-to-basics movement has supporters among both blacks and whites, several of the other attacks against public and higher education are motivated to a greater or lesser extent by the factors of race and economic disadvantage. These issues play a role in the continuing defeat of school levies in urban areas, the continuing opposition to busing, the clamor for tuition tax credits and education vouchers for parents, and mounting opposition to spending for the economically and educationally disadvantaged. These issues are often interrelated, as an individual could oppose increased spending for schools, particularly when it is perceived that the beneficiaries are often black and poor; could oppose court-ordered busing and support tuition tax credits and education vouchers as alternatives to or escapes from busing.

Over the past few years there has been growing opposition among white voters to supporting increased school tax levies. In some cities the defeats have been sparked by declining enrollments in the schools. In other cities race is clearly an issue as white voters do not wish to pay increased school taxes for school systems in the process of becoming "blacker" or facing possible desegregation. Although black students made up one-third of the students in Toledo, Ohio schools, white voters, largely on the grounds of race, defeated a school bond issue.[13] In Detroit, white voters unsuccessfully opposed an increased school tax levy for the largely black public school system.[14] In Ohio cities such as Cincinnati, Cleveland, Columbus, and Dayton white voters have repeatedly defeated school bond levies in attempts to forestall court-ordered desegregation.[15]

At the same time, the imposition of court-ordered busing, designed to redress the past and present inequities in terms of racial composition of schools, still incurs the wrath of parents. Opposition to using the public schools as "laboratories for experimentation" has led many parents to move to suburban areas or to enroll their children in parochial and private schools. While many parents profess that these moves were not the result of racial considerations, but a pursuit of "quality education," a recent study of parental behavior and attitudes suggests otherwise. Based upon analysis of respondents to public opinion polls, the authors conclude "it is apparently the *symbolism* evoked by the prospect of *any* white children's forced intimate contact with blacks, rather than the *reality* of one's *own* children's contact, that triggers opposition to busing."[16]

At the same time, an increased number of citizens are questioning the current level of spending for education. Although a recent poll shows that a majority of Americans (85.2 percent) believe that "too little" (51.6 percent) or "about right" (33.6 percent) is being spent on education,[17] the public mood to cut taxes, as exemplified by Proposition 13, affects the current level of spending for schools. Moreover, an increasing number of parents and educators are questioning the present allocation of funds. Some contend, as does one educator, that billions of dollars are spent in behalf of educating "the handicapped and the mediocre" at the expense of "brains and excellence."[18] This same turning away from the needs of the educationally disadvantaged sparked the decision of a middle-class school district in Queens to turn down federal funds for after-school jobs. Since the funds were earmarked for more needy black youngsters bused into the district rather than for the relatively comfortable middle-class youths, the parents rejected the funds.[19]

Having briefly presented the arguments of those who oppose increased funding for schools and for educational programs for blacks and the educationally

disadvantaged, the next chapters examine how the continued opposition to busing, the possible implementation of tuition tax credit and education vouchers,
and the implementation of competency based testing programs serve to hinder
equal educational opportunity for blacks.

6

The Opposition
to Busing

Unlike earlier years when the imposition of busing by federal courts was greeted by acts of violence, the physical resistance to busing within the past two years has been far less noticeable. Instead of the burning of school buses in Pontiac, Michigan; the stoning of buses carrying black children to school in Lamar, South Carolina; and the numerous incidents of racial violence in Boston, there have been far fewer acts of violence as a result of the imposition of busing during the past two school years. The tensions in Boston and Louisville, the sites of much of the anti-busing violence and furor during the mid-1970s, have quieted down. This is not to suggest increased public tolerance of busing, but perhaps begrudging public acceptance of busing.

But opposition to busing continues, although the nature of that opposition has changed. The physical confrontations between the supporters and opponents of busing have declined. Certainly the recent demonstrations and protests against the imposition of busing in Los Angeles do not compare to those held in Boston. Instead, one witnesses the debate and confrontation among scholars and congressmen over busing. Within the past two years there have been charges and counter-charges, accusations and counter-accusations, studies and rebuttals over the merits of busing. During the same period, several pieces of anti-busing legislation, including one proposed constitutional amendment, have been introduced and debated in Congress.

Critics of busing cite various arguments in support of their opposition. Basically they agree that the original intent of the Supreme Court in the *Brown* decision has been fulfilled.[1] Some contend, as do law professor Lino A. Graglia, economist Thomas Sowell, and sociologist Nathan Glazer, that the present court-ordered busing is another example of the federal judiciary's blatant abuse of power.[2] Sowell also points to public opinion polls as indicators of black opposition to busing.[3] Although most public opinion polls show that a majority and/or a plurality of black Americans approve of busing, there is not a monolithic position in support of busing within the black community.[4] However, the views of black spokespersons who oppose further court-ordered busing do differ from the critics such as Glazer and Sowell. Harvard Law Professor Derrick Bell has emerged as one of the leading opponents of further court-ordered busing. Bell argues in support of improving the quality of education for urban blacks through increased funding and increased parental involvement.[5] While a strain of similarity may be found in the arguments of Sowell and Glazer, particularly in their guarded and limited endorsement of the concept of community control, Bell advocates that the courts order the spending of more money to upgrade predominantly black schools.[6] The spending of *more* money for urban education, particularly as ordered by a member of the "imperial judiciary," is not a position publicly supported by most traditional critics of busing. Moreover, both Glazer and Sowell advocate diversity and pluralism in education, words implying support for tuition tax credits for private and parochial schools and vouchers. That position puts them squarely at odds with those blacks who, while opposing busing, advocate increased black participation in and control of public school systems, not through vouchers.[7]

The core of the most recent arguments against court-ordered busing centers around those raised by sociologist James Coleman, educator Diane Ravitch and sociologist David Armor. These scholars contend that busing mandated by the federal courts increases "white flight." To escape or to avoid having their children bused to schools to achieve racial balance, they argue, white parents will *flee* from urban areas under desegregation orders to suburban areas. Thus, these scholars conclude, mandatory busing is counterproductive as it results in the further loss of white students from urban school systems, and leads to "resegregation" or further racial isolation.[8]

Professor Christine Rossell has emerged as one of the leading critics of the white flight thesis. She recognizes that court-ordered school desegregation does lead to white flight, especially during the first year of implementation. However, she maintains, the effect of white flight is short-term, for between the third and fifth years of busing plans there are "less than normal white enrollment losses." Moreover, she attributes the decline in the number of white students in urban school systems not solely to school desegregation, but also to the trend to suburbanization prior to any court-ordered desegregation and to the declining birth rate among whites.[9]

There is a clear link between housing in urban areas and white flight that needs to be explored. The city of Chicago has experienced a 40 percent decrease in white enrollment in its school system from 1968 to 1976. If one were to assume white flight as a prime factor, then how does one account for the fact that Chicago has over ninety elementary schools with less than 10 per cent minority enrollment?[10] But the decrease in housing units among whites declined far more than the number of white students. Thus, dissatisfaction with the public schools cannot be the major reason for white flight from Chicago.[11]

To curb white flight, the critics, especially Diane Ravitch, advocate ''a cautious and deliberate approach'' to avoid resegregation.[12] Such an approach would call for the implementation of voluntary busing plans, inter-district voluntary transfers, educational vouchers, and a system of incentives.[13] In some instances, implementation of the Ravitch suggestions has been carried out. However, the widespread use of these suggestions appears to be far too limited to serve as effective alternatives to busing.

Although Armor hails the success of voluntary busing in San Diego as a means of promoting desegregation while not bringing about massive white flight,[14] one needs to study the mechanics of voluntary busing. It is true that the white enrollment in San Diego declined by only 2.2 percent over the past year, but white children are not volunteering to desegregate schools. Out of 10,500 San Diego children involved in the Voluntary Ethnic Enrollment Program, only twenty were white.[15] Resentment of the onesidedness of voluntary desegregation, a common complaint of black parents, was expressed by a San Diego Urban League official who remarked:

> Black parents ought to rethink their participation in this program. There's always been some rumblings about why do I keep on volunteering when whites aren't doing it.[16]

Similar resentment against the burden assumed by minority youngsters in voluntary busing plans was expressed in a recent report submitted by a court-appointed committee monitoring school desegregation in Los Angeles. Of 18, 360 children enrolled in the voluntary busing program, Permits With Transportation, only 165 are white.[17] Nor did this voluntary plan help to curb white flight in Los Angeles, as that city lost 15 percent of its white population. Thus, voluntary busing is not as effective a solution as its supporters allege. On the one hand, it places too great a burden on minority youngsters to bring about desegregation. At the same time it is not a sure-fire guarantee to prevent white flight.

Nor does the implementation of inter-district voluntary transfer seem to be an effective solution, for it too results only in token desegregation. Moreover, the critics' support of educational vouchers, to be discussed later, poses far more danger to the concept of public school education than it does to assuring quality education. And, as in the proposal turned down by the Hammond, Indiana school board, educational incentives can be viewed as bribes. To thwart a proposed

NAACP suit calling for the implementation of busing, one school board member unsuccessfully proposed the awarding of a $500 yearly credit toward college costs or toward a down payment on a home to each student in Hammond volunteering to attend an integrated school.[18]

Aside from its critics in academia, members of Congress have regularly assailed busing. Since 1974 Congress has passed three amendments to legislation, the Esch, Byrd, and Eagleton-Biden amendments, in attempts to curb federal ordering or enforcement of busing. These amendments, according to the United States Commission on Civil Rights, have helped to thwart "the ability of the executive and judicial branches to guarantee the nation's children and young people their constitutional rights."[19] Perhaps the House of Representatives' recent defeat of a proposed constitutional amendment against busing signals a new attitude in Congress toward busing. The bulk of support for the amendment came from parts of the Northeast and Midwest. On the other hand, some Southern congressmen who have witnessed the anti-busing fervor and its decline in their states, voted against the amendment.[20]

While the critics contend that busing leads to white flight and is unpopular among both blacks and whites, evidence suggests otherwise. There are numerous towns and cities, often out of the national spotlight, where busing is working. Moreover, cities that once were hotbeds of anti-busing fervor and activity are now calmer and are reporting gains in education as a result of busing. In Louisville, Kentucky, the site of anti-busing rallies three years ago, white flight is not a major problem. And although interracial contact is still minimal, black and white students are learning to get along. More importantly, the grades of black students have improved.[21] Similar findings have been reported elsewhere. In Charlotte, North Carolina the achievement scores of black students have improved, the dropout rate has declined, and the percentage of black students going on to college has risen.[22]

Even the public school system of Boston, the 1970's symbol of defiance and resistance to court-ordered desegregation of public schools, is now experiencing gains as a result of busing. Jonathan Kozol, author of *Death at an Early Age* and a long time critic of the public school system in Boston, has noted that since the implementation of busing, Boston schools have moved from "scholastic mediocrity to educational distinction."[23] More importantly, the rate of college attendance among South Boston's graduates has risen since the implementation of busing.[24] Among the recent educational innovations resulting from Judge W. Arthur Garrity's order have been the creation of magnet schools for the arts and sciences, environmental studies, aviation and medicine. Although critics of busing often cite the attractiveness of magnet schools as alternatives to court-ordered desegregation, the schools' successes have been most apparent in areas—Boston and Dallas for example—where they have been created as a result of court-ordered desegregation.[25]

These accounts, often little noticed by the critics of busing, are indeed encouraging and illustrate how busing can work when a community—black parents, white parents, city officials, involved citizens—and the school make a concerted effort to see that busing is given a chance and the proper climate in which to work.

The educational gains in Louisville, Charlotte and Boston are not isolated examples. A recent review of seventy-three studies of the effects of desegregation on the achievement of black students by Robert Crain and Rita Mahard found that in a majority of cases school desegregation has had a positive impact on the test scores of black students. Forty studies recorded increases in the test scores, while only twelve indicated negative results.[26] Moreover, in direct response to the arguments of Armor and Coleman, Crain and Mahard found that mandatory busing programs tended to produce more positive results than voluntary plans. Because mandatory programs often involve more planning for their implementation, they are likely to result in more community involvement, more "soul searching" and innovation by the school district.[27] Based on a review and analysis of 29 studies of mandatory desegregation plans in the North and South, the authors found twenty-four reporting gains in achievement for blacks, while only five reported losses.[28]

Public opinion polls continue to show opposition by most whites to busing. In some instances, when alternatives, such as changing school boundaries or building low income housing in middle-class neighborhoods, are presented, blacks also oppose busing.[29] The latter measures are not surprising, for busing is just one of several strategies that could be used to bring about school desegregation. However, in the absence or failure of local jurisdictions to redistrict school boundaries or to encourage the building of "scatter-site" housing, busing remains one of the few vehicles to bring about meaningful desegregation of public school systems. Blacks do recognize the viability of busing for, in the absence of alternatives, poll after poll reveal black support of busing. Watts and Free found that 69 percent of the blacks surveyed expressed support of busing, mandatory or voluntary.[30] A recent review of National Opinion Research Center surveys from 1972–1977 indicates that a majority of blacks support busing.[31] A recently released poll of black southerners, commissioned by the *Atlanta Constitution,* found that 57 percent favor busing as a means of achieving racial integration.[32] More revealing are the responses of the parents of bused children. It is this group of parents, both black and white, who should be able to offer the best endorsements or indictments of busing. Eighty-eight percent of black parents found busing to be a "very satisfactory" or "partly satisfactory" experience. Seventy-nine percent of the white parents gave the same response. When asked why, these parents reported "No problems, no complaints from children;" "Children learn more, better school;" "Children learn to live with each other;" and "no fighting or trouble."[33] Commenting on this situation, pollster Lou Harris notes:

> The irony of busing to achieve racial balance is that rarely has there been a case where so many have been opposed to an idea, which appears not to work badly at all when put into practice, at least from the testimony of families who have lived through the experience.[34]

How then does one assess racial integration in public schools twenty-five years after the *Brown* decision, particularly in regard to busing? The implementation and execution of busing as a strategy to bring about school desegregation has been mixed. Busing's successes have been more clearly noted in the southern states where public schools are now the least segregated and where educational gains are being recorded. These gains should not overshadow the loss of black role models—black principals and black teachers. At the same time, there has been continuous footdragging, particularly in the North and in the West, to bring about the desegregation of public school systems. The Supreme Court's two recent decisions, *Columbus Board of Education* v. *Penick* and *Dayton Board of Education* v. *Brinkman*, upheld busing orders for these two cities as "affirmative duty" to correct and eliminate the effects of past discrimination of school boards.[35] These decisions hopefully will signal the Burger Court's commitment to end racial segregation in northern school systems. Although it is too early to predict the impact of these cases on future litigation or future events, it is hoped that an attitude of compliance, rather than one of white flight, will be adopted by the citizens of Columbus and Dayton. Should the latter be adopted, that attitude should not be used as a device to limit or to evade the meaning of the *Brown* decision.

7

Tuition Tax Credits
and
Education Vouchers

Over the course of the past few years, families with children at or nearing college age have been concerned with the spiraling costs of college attendance, particularly at the more prestigious, private institutions. While costs at public institutions average $2,346, costs at several of the Ivy League institutions exceed or will soon exceed $8,000 per year.[1] Analyses of these costs reveal that since the mid-1960s they have risen by 74.2 percent at public institutions and by 76 percent at private institutions.[2] But, according to a Congressional Budget Office study, these rising costs have been outpaced by the rise in family median income. Income for families with children in college rose by 87.3 percent.[3] The following chart compares the overall increase in college costs at public and private institutions to the increased median income.

Moreover, as the chart clearly shows, college costs consume just slightly less of a family's budget than they did a decade ago. But are college costs so intolerable or are there changing public attitudes, particularly among the middle-and upper-middle classes, about the financing of higher education? As an increasing number of middle-and upper-income parents and students are questioning the value of college attendance, many are now more reluctant to assume the financial costs. According to a College Entrance Examination Board study of applications for federal student aid, there were "substantial differences between ability and willingness" of parents to pay for the costs of college education.[4] This changed

TABLE 2

College Costs *vs*. Family Income

Year	Median Income All Families	Median Income Families with 18-24 Year Olds	Tuition, Fees, Room, Board Public Colleges	Tuition, Fees, Room, Board Private Colleges	Percent of Median Income (Families with 18-24 Year Olds) Public Colleges	Percent of Median Income (Families with 18-24 Year Olds) Private Colleges	Consumer Price Index 1967 = 100
1967	$6,811	$7,923	$1,063	$2,205	13.4%	27.8%	100.0
1970	8,268	9,624	1,288	2,739	13.4	28.5	116.3
1973	10,273	11,897	1,517	3,164	12.8	26.6	133.1
1974	11,025	12,561	1,617	3,386	12.9	27.0	147.7
1975	11,505	13,199	1,748	3,667	13.2	27.8	161.2
1976	12,199	14,164	1,854	3,896	13.1	27.5	170.5

Percent Change from 1967 to 1976

	79.1%	78.8%	74.2%	76.7%	−2.3%	−1.1%	70.5%

SOURCE: Congressional Budget Office, from the *Washington Post*, 3 May 1978, P. A5.

attitude of "is college worth it", emerging among many parents, has been aptly summed up by an unnamed college official who has stated:

> (e)arly in the 20th century a college education for your child was an insurance policy . . . Make your kid a doctor and he'll support you. Now parents don't want to be dependent in that way.[5]

Although data do indicate that rising college costs have not exceeded the increase in family median income, the cries of middle- and upper-income families have led to sympathetic portrayals in the media and a receptive response from Congress. During the last session of Congress, the House and the Senate, in another response to the "middle-class revolt" considered tuition tax credits for the parents, spouses, or individuals enrolled in institutions of higher education. As part of the tuition tax credit legislation, Congress considered providing tax credits to the parents of children enrolled in private and parochial schools. Senators Robert Packwood and Daniel Moynihan introduced legislation which would provide tax credits to individual taxpayers of 50 percent of tuition payments up to five hundred dollars per student.

Tuition tax credit legislation has been heralded by its supporters as providing tax relief to an inflation-weary and tax-burdened middle class. However, this legislation poses serious threats to the attainment of equal opportunity in education for blacks. On one hand, tax credit legislation designed to relieve the alleged plight of the middle-income and upper-income, threatens funding for lower-income students, many of whom are black. Equally disturbing are the threats posed by allowing tax credits for the parents of parochial and private school students; for, if tuition tax credits for these parents are enacted, they will present a serious, perhaps damaging, threat to the very nature and concept of public school education.

As the congressional debate over tuition tax credits revealed, the prime beneficiaries of tuition tax credits would be upper-income families. It has been estimated that 46 percent of the benefits of tuition tax credits would go to those families whose yearly incomes exceed $25,000.[6] But the median family incomes of most black students attending college are not high enough for them to benefit from tax credits. Over sixty percent of black students are from families having yearly incomes of less than $10,000. Consequently, tax credits would be of little use to most black students and their families.[7]

Congress, in place of the Packwood-Moynihan bill, passed the Middle Income Student Aid Act (MISA). Under the provisions of this act, the upper limit for eligibility for Basic Educational Opportunity Grants (BEOGs) was extended to $25,000, making an estimated 1.5 million more students eligible for BEOGs. In addition, more monies and larger awards were to be awarded to those students whose family incomes were below $15,000. However, by raising the family income level for eligibility, MISA allows middle-income students to take advantage of BEOGs without necessarily ensuring equality of opportunity.[8]

The most controversial aspect of the proposed tuition tax credit legislation is the provision to provide tax relief to the parents of private and parochial school students. To a large extent the debate has centered around the constitutional argument of separation of church and state. Congressional opponents argue that tax credits to private schools will largely benefit the parents of children in Catholic elementary and secondary schools, thus providing governmental aid to religious educational institutions.[9] Its supporters argue that this type of credit does not violate the Constitution, would increase parental choice in selecting the type of schools for their children, and would encourage educational diversity in the types of institutions available.[10]

Economists Thomas Sowell and Walter Williams view tuition tax credits as providing invaluable educational alternatives to urban blacks. Noting the increased black enrollment nationwide in parochial schools, both contend that tuition tax credits would allow more blacks to take advantage of that option. Moreover, they profess, as does James Coleman, that tax credits would help stem white flight from urban school districts, particularly those undergoing court-ordered desegregation, and would encourage the voluntary racial integration of private schools.[11]

At first glance, the arguments of Sowell and Williams might seem plausible. Indeed, an increasing number of black youngsters, often non-Catholics, are enrolled in parochial schools. However, the number of parochial schools in inner cities is declining, not necessarily due to declining enrollments, but due to decreasing commitment to their continued existence by the Catholic Church. According to the National Office for Black Catholics (NOBC), the hierarchy of the Church is closing inner-city schools while commiting more funds to schools in suburban parishes. One reason for the closings, suggests the NOBC, is the increased enrollment of non-Catholics.[12] It is particularly ironic that supporters of tax credits would ask the federal government via tax credits to help finance parochial school education inasmuch as the Catholic Church has shown a decreasing commitment to the continued existence of many of these schools.

However, tuition tax credits, rather than increasing the educational options available to parents, particularly black and low-income parents, pose a grave threat to the present concept and historic intent of public education. Repeatedly, the supporters of tuition tax credits argue that the availability of educational alternatives would force public schools to improve through increased competition for students.[13] However, rather than forcing public schools to improve, tuition tax credits would more than likely threaten their continued existence. As numerous black leaders and spokesmen have acknowledged, increased enrollment in private and parochial schools would lead to declining public interest and concern for public schools. Vernon Jordan maintains that tuition tax credits offer "incentives to desert public schools at the very time when those public schools need more aid to improve their services."[14] Benjamin Mays, former president of Morehouse College and currently President of the Atlanta Board of Education, on a more somber note, writes:

> (i)f and when our public schools become mostly Black, city, state and federal governments will neglect them. This will be a tragedy of the first magnitude.[15]

Bayard Rustin, likewise, argues that tuition tax credits pose a threat to public schools, particularly in terms of the redistribution and reallocation of funds for public education. Such acts, he maintains, will lead to the creation of a two-tiered educational system in this country—public schools for the poor and dispossessed, many of whom are black, and private schools for the affluent.[16]

Nor judging from experience does it seem likely that tuition tax credits would discourage white middle-class flight from urban school systems. According to a recent Johns Hopkins study, white enrollment in private and parochial schools was and is closely related to the black percentage of the population in a given city. Over the past two decades, cities with large black populations have witnessed increasing white enrollment in private and parochial schools.[17] According to Henry Becker, director of the study, tuition tax credits "may result in greater social-class and racial segregation of American children than now exists." For, he maintains, tax credits might be "more widely used by white families in cities with large or growing black populations, and could inhibit progress on school desegregation in these cities."[18]

Supporters of public school education, a wide and varied coalition of civil rights organizations, teacher organizations, organized labor and other groups, successfully lobbied to prevent congressional passage of tuition tax credit legislation for the parents of children in private and parochial schools. However, Senator Moynihan has once again introduced such legislation. While the fate of such legislation is still uncertain, there are signs that such legislation is unconstitutional. The Supreme Court, in affirming a Federal Appeals Court ruling in *Byrne v. Public Funds for Public Schools,* struck down a New Jersey law allowing income tax deductions of $1,000 per pupil to the parents of children attending non-public schools on the grounds that the law was in violation of the First Amendment.[19] While the implications of this decision on the pending legislation have not been fully treated in the media, one account has noted that the decision has been the "strongest signal yet to Congress and state legislatures that the Constitution is a barrier to aid to parochial schools below the college level."[20]

Education Vouchers

A more radical extension of the tuition tax credit argument is the revival of the argument for education vouchers. As conceived by voucher supporters, local and/or state governments would not directly fund public school systems as they currently do. Rather, the sums appropriated for the education of each individual child would go to the parents of that child in the form of a certificate or voucher. In turn, parents would use these vouchers to pay the school, public or private, they wish to have their child attend.[21] According to its proponents, as diverse a group as Milton Friedman and Thomas Sowell and Christopher Jencks, vouchers would allow parents to have far greater latitude and choice in determining how and where their children are educated. Moreover, they assert, vouchers eliminate the "monopoly" of the public school systems by providing "competition" to the public schools. This competition via the free market, they allege, can only prove to be beneficial as the quality of schooling would improve through innovation and diversity. In addition, vouchers would force individual schools to be more concerned with the educational needs of students and with the demands of parents. For, if parents are dissatisfied with an individual school, they can withdraw their child.[22]

These arguments, more than a decade old, are currently being revived in a new wave of social science literature. Some of this literature pertains to re-assessments of the implementation of vouchers in the Alum Rock California School district. The Alum Rock experiment with vouchers, based largely upon a plan proposed by

Christopher Jencks and others, and funded in part by the Office of Economic Opportunity, was a "transition" voucher program involving only some of the public schools in the largely minority populated school system of Alum Rock.[23] In each of the voucher schools, "mini-schools" were set up emphasizing different educational programs such as enrichment programs and bilingual/bicultural programs. A preliminary assessment of the Alum Rock experiment, conducted one year after its inception by the Rand Corporation, found mixed results.[24] While "mini-schools" did offer educational choices to parents, the focus of power under decentralization shifted from educational administrators to teachers. Moreover, very few students transferred during the first year. Thus, vouchers did not encourage voluntary school desegregation inasmuch as Alum Rock was already one of the more desegregated cities in the nation prior to the voucher experiment.[25]

More recent assessments of Alum Rock generally agree with the findings of the earlier Rand study. A 1977 assessment by David K. Cohen and Eleanor Farrar notes that vouchers did not quite lead to the results anticipated by its supporters. Vouchers, they maintain, led both to more choice for parents and to increasing power for teachers and administrators. Although sympathetic to the concept of vouchers, they conclude that the voucher concept "was simply based on a serious overestimate of popular discontent and the demand for change in education."[26] Based upon a similar review of the Alum Rock experiment, another study contends that vouchers can help bring about the desegregation of schools.[27] However, a review of the data cited does not necessarily support that conclusion. Although the overall percentage of black, Spanish-surnamed and white students enrolled in voucher and non-voucher schools in Alum Rock remained fairly constant, this finding should not be attributed to vouchers. Only eight percent of the students in Alum Rock made use of the vouchers, thus the previous racial balance in Alum Rock was not greatly disturbed.[28]

Nevertheless, sparred by the perceived failings of the public school system, increased parental desires for educational choice and parental fears of school desegregation, the concepts of vouchers in theory, (not as practiced in Alum Rock) have become more popular. A recent book, *Education by Choice: The Case for Family Control* by Professors John E. Coons and Stephen D. Sugarman has whetted much of this interest.[29] Based upon the book's thesis—increased family control over a child's education—Coons and Sugarman are spearheading a campaign in California to establish a statewide system of vouchers. Their initiative, the "Family Choice in Education," would allow all school-age children to be eligible for vouchers to be used in public and private schools in the state. At the same time, the initiative would place a ceiling on spending on education within the state. If successful, this initiative could pose a death blow to public school education. On the one hand, public schools in California, the possible victims of declining funds as a result of Proposition 13, would have to compete with private schools for already limited monies via vouchers. Moreover, would parental choice via vouchers deter middle-income families from fleeing urban and suburban school systems? If the experiences surrounding the establishment of "segregation academies" may serve as an example, vouchers may enhance white flight, leaving the public school system to serve primarily minorities and the poor. Nor are there any real guarantees, other than the speculations of its supporters that vouchers would bring about "stable and enduring" forms of voluntary school integration.[30] As witnessed by the successful lobbying campaign waged by parents and administrators of racially segregated private schools, Congress has delayed an Internal Revenue Service proposal to deny tax-exempt status to these schools, without an effective means of guaranteeing voluntary school integration. Thus, the parental choice advocated by voucher supporters may lead to racial exclusion in the guise of pluralism—a far cry from stable and enduring school integration.

8

Competency Based Testing

One of the more sensitive and controversial aspects of the "back to basics" movement is that of competency based testing. Spurred by heavy criticism and countless attacks, and by the occasional lawsuits that allege that school districts are graduating "functional illiterates," close to forty state systems of public education have rushed to implement competency based testing as a means of reversing this trend. Although the particulars of competency based testing differ from state to state, generally it follows either one or two procedures. To curb "social promotion," school systems may require a student to pass state tests in reading and mathematics at selected grade intervals in school. However, as presently understood by most, competency based testing entails a student's passing of standardized tests in reading and mathematics before he or she receives a high school diploma. If a high school student, after having up to three or four opportunities to pass the tests by the end of the senior year, still is unable to pass the tests, he or she will not be awarded a diploma but a certificate of attendance.

As is evident by its rather rapid acceptance and use across the country, competency based testing has struck a responsive chord among many, particularly among parents and employers who bemoan declining test and achievement scores and literacy skills. But competency based testing movements are being implemented by the state systems of education at the same time that more and more arguments are being raised against standardized tests. Increasingly, black parents and interested parties have filed suits against the use of IQ tests and other standardized tests for placement within schools. They have argued that a disproportionate number of black students who score low on these tests have been placed in special education and mentally educable classes. Yet, the very same students receive higher scores, often significantly higher, on less biased tests.[1] Moreover, educators are becoming increasingly skeptical of just what skills and abilities tests do measure.[2] An ISEP study of testing states what more and more educators and policy makers have come to realize:

> ... test scores alone frequently are not sufficient measures of aptitude or other psychological constructs for minority groups.[3]

Although doubts about testing have increased in recent years, proponents of competency based testing maintain that such tests help to identify student deficiencies and weaknesses, to establish minimum standards of competency, and to increase the morale of students and teachers.[4] Yet the tests raise serious but still largely unanswered questions: What is the definition of competency? What is minimal competency? How does one test minimal competency?[5] Education critics of the tests take its proponents to task for not clearly defining competency— mastery of "basic skills" taught in school or mastery of "life skills," those not taught in school. They also criticize the arbitrary definition of minimum as what is plausible to expect and politically tolerable to accept.[6]

Although doubts about the tests remain, newspaper accounts of the spread of competency based testing stress both their appeal and their "minimum effects."[7] However, the effects of competency based testing upon blacks can hardly be viewed as minimum. Rather, the tests, as currently structured and used, portend far-reaching and largely negative consequences for blacks. This is not to suggest that blacks are anti-competence, for a repeated cry among black parents and black educators has been to stress the basic skills.[8] But blacks clearly recognize the inherent biases and inadequacies present in allegedly neutral tests. Black parents do question the current timing in implementing these tests. In some recently desegregated school districts, black parents contend that competency based testing did not become a major issue in their communities and in their schools until the schools were desegregated. Lower test results for black students, they insist, have led to all-black and all-white classes within supposedly integrated schools.[9]

More disturbing have been the preliminary results of black students, particularly those in high schools, on competency based tests. When first given to high school juniors in Florida in 1977, just under one fourth (23 percent) of black students passed the math section while nearly three-fourths (74 percent) passed the English section.[10] Although more recent figures show a slight improvement, they do not suggest any reason for optimism: forty percent of the black students passed the math section while 89 percent passed the English examination.[11] As these numbers suggest, it is clear that substantial numbers of black youngsters may not receive high school diplomas, but certificates of attendance. Coupled with the already high dropout rate of black students, those students failing competency based tests would only decrease the number of black students who would be able to pursue post-secondary education. And with the national unemployment rate for black teenagers exceeding 30 percent, these youngsters would stand little chance of securing jobs.

The recent decision in federal district court in Florida to postpone for four years the passing of a competency based test as a requirement for graduation, does offer some consolation. Although upholding the test as valid and reliable, the judge delayed the use of the test until the "taint of segregation" has been removed from Florida's school system.[12] What must be done is to use competency based tests not as "exit exams" designed to classify an individual's life chances, but as diagnostic tests given in elementary schools to indicate a student's weaknesses. Thus, as Vernon Jordan, Jesse Jackson, Carl Rowan and Mary Berry have suggested, monies and effort must be expended to bring about remediation.[13]

9

Proposition 13 and the Tax Revolt

If any one event symbolizes the emergent American mood of self-interest and indifference and/or hostility toward the well-being of the total society, perhaps it has been the passage of the Jarvis-Gann initiative, better known as Proposition 13, by the voters of California in June of 1978. By almost a two-to-one margin, Californians voted to reduce the property tax rate on homes and businesses from two percent to one percent. In effect, Californians voted to reduce their property taxes from $12 billion to $5 billion, a 57 percent reduction.

Economist Paul Samuelson has termed the passage of Proposition 13 as "the most important U.S. political-economic event of 1978, perhaps even of the 1970s."[1] His description of the impact of Proposition 13 should not be considered an overstatement. The voters of California have fueled the spread of a nationwide "tax revolt" against property taxes, state income taxes and sale taxes. Moreover, the passage of Proposition 13 has led both the Congress and the president to attempt to outvie each other in their pronouncements to reduce federal spending. In addition, close to thirty state legislatures, again sparked by Proposition 13, have passed resolutions calling for the convening of a constitutional convention to require a balanced federal budget.

Has the furor against government in general and government spending in particular been wholly justified? When one compares government spending in this country with that of six European nations, the grievances against both government spending and taxation look less convincing. As the figures in Table 3 indicate, citizens of the United States enjoy, by a relatively comfortable margin,

57

TABLE 3

Comparative Percentage of Government
Spending for Seven Nations

Nation	Spending as Percentage of Output	Taxes as Percentage of Earnings
Denmark	46	33
Germany	47	27
Netherlands	55	31
Norway	51	27
Sweden	62	35
United Kingdom	44	26
United States	33	17

SOURCE: Robert J. Samuelson. "The New Ideology." *National Journal* 10 (21 October 1978):1686.

both the lowest rate of government spending as a percentage of national output and the lowest rate of taxation than do the citizens of these respective nations.[2]

Likewise, the middle class has profited from government services, programs and activities. To paraphrase an argument by Eric Goldman, the "self-made" middle class overlooks the benefits they have received from government financed mortages, the G.I. bill and other federal aid to higher education, federal construction of highways, and federally funded jobs. Underlying much of this hostility to government spending is the belief of many individuals that spending for programs should be geared to the particular benefits they may accrue. Columnist George F. Will points out the ironies of this preoccupation with individual selfishness. "Today's conservatism is," he writes, "primarily the idea that government should cut my neighbor's subsidy."[3]

While Proposition 13 was directed specifically against the property tax in California, the 2 percent tax rate there was not overly excessive, rather it was approximately the national average. Moreover, California homeowners paid proportionately more in state income taxes and in sales taxes than through the property taxes.[4] But the presence of the property tax was a convenient vehicle for Californians to vent their anger at the spiraling cost of homes, the failure of the California state legislature to pass a form of tax relief, and the presence of a five billion dollar surplus in the state treasury.[5]

Proposition 13 has been defended by its supporters as a middle-class revolt against rising taxes and waste in government.[6] However, the measure should be viewed as an expression and manifestation of narrow individual and class interests, motivated in large part by greed and race. Contending that the passage of Proposition 13 was not racist, Jarvis has asserted rather boldly that the measure "will help minorities more than anything else has."[7] However, black voters in California did not then and still do not share Jarvis' assessment. Black voters opposed Proposition 13 by a 67 percent to 33 percent margin. Once the measure was enacted, blacks were the only major bloc still opposed to Proposition 13, 61 percent to 34 percent.[8] Although some have attributed class and economic interests, or an increasing conservatism to the voting patterns and behavior of blacks supporting the initiative, nonetheless, a solid majority of black voters saw the need for continued government spending for social services.[9]

Perhaps the most salient commentary on the motivation and rationale behind the passage of Proposition 13 was a *New Republic* editorial entitled "Me First." According to the editorial, Proposition 13:

> ... was not just a cause for property owners to join, but a fight on principle against flabby government. We suspect that this blending of libertarian rhetoric with cash prizes for the middle class is the central appeal of the new backlash that is gaining momentum in the country. It salves the conscience by saying that voters can do good by doing well for themselves, even if doing so means that they withdraw from the community.[10]

Matching both the tone and substance of the *New Republic* argument, Vernon Jordan states:

> (s)tripped to its essentials, the tax revolt represents a shell game, in which middle class voters fall for meat axe slashes in taxes that benefit the rich while saving a few pennies for themselves, if that, and reducing the public services that benefit the poor.[11]

These assessments accurately gauge the declining public commitment to the public good and the emergent overconcern with self-interest. For, in passing Proposition 13, Californians have voted to provide fewer social services for themselves and for those who need them the most—blacks, other minorities and the poor. This mean-spiritedness is reflected in what social services Californians see fit to cut. According to a *Los Angeles Times*/CBS news poll conducted among those voting in California, 69 percent supported cuts in welfare payments.[12] The spirit of much of this anti-welfare sentiment directed against the poor can be seen in comments expressed by Howard Jarvis. According to Jarvis, the Constitution does not guarantee either "life, liberty and welfare or life, liberty and food stamps."[13] Contrary to the demagoguery of Jarvis, this massive anti-welfare sentiment, at the heart of much of the pro-Proposition 13 arguments, is not and will not be resolved by the reduction of property taxes. For, the funding of most public assistance programs comes from the state and federal governments, not from local governments.

Although Proposition 13 has not reduced social services as much as feared, its potential impact should not be overlooked. There have been cutbacks in social services, particularly those used by the poor. Counties have had to cut some services to the poor by reducing caseloads. In Orange County, reduced staffing in services used by the poor and low-income families has resulted in cuts in child abuse programs and protective services for children and foster home programs.[14] And while public assistance payments have not been reduced, they face reduction should a planned initiative to reduce the state income tax be passed.[15]

The state employees who have been laid off, have usually been low-level employees such as janitors and clerks.[16] Thus, it is the unskilled and semi-skilled workers, many of whom are black, Chicano and the working poor who are suffering the brunt of the cutbacks. The current freeze on the hiring of public employees will impact upon minorities. One incident was the picture of two black policemen in Oakland who were given dismissal notices one half hour after graduating from the Police Academy.[17] Aside from this one instance, Proposition 13 and the current campaign to reduce the state income tax, pose threats to the future availability of jobs in the public sector. Much of the economic progress achieved by blacks has been made in the public sector.[18] However, cutbacks in the availability of public sector jobs will reduce or stymie many of these gains. According to data compiled by economist Andrew Brimmer, in 1975 blacks held 9.5 percent of the jobs in this country. Of these jobs, 9.2 percent were in the private sector while 16.2 percent and 12.9 percent were in the federal and state and local governments, respectively.[19] Brimmer notes: "(t)he heavy dependence of blacks on public sector jobs was cast into sharp relief by the cutback in state and local government mandated by the passage of Proposition 13."[20] An increasing number of recent black college graduates are reporting difficulty in finding employment in the public sector because of the imposition of hiring freezes.[21]

Moreover, should future cutbacks in public sector employment be made in California, the experiences of black public employees in New York City during its fiscal crisis in 1975–1976 do not serve as pleasant precedents. The adage "last-hired, first fired" unfortunately held true as a disproportionate percentage of those teachers, policemen and firemen laid off in New York City were black.

However, one vital service heavily dependent upon funding from property taxes is education. It is education, from kindergarten through the graduate level, that may bear an undue share of the reduced funding. Although Proposition 13 was passed just over two years ago, it is still too early to provide a detailed assessment of the full ramifications of its passage. Preliminary signs, particularly in its impact on public education and public higher education in California, are not encouraging. Perhaps least encouraging has been reduced funding, even with federal and increased state aid, for the public school system statewide. Even with the infusion of $2 billion in aid from the state surplus, public schools in California did receive fewer funds this year than last.[22] As a result, summer school sessions were eliminated in Los Angeles and San Diego. Moreover, teaching positions were eliminated; some through attrition and others through layoffs. According to a survey conducted by the State Department of Education, over one half of the school districts responding, 60 out of 114, had fewer teachers in 1978–1979 than during the previous year.[23] While most assessments give the impression that the reduced teaching staffs are the results of attrition and a state imposed hiring freeze, 54 percent of teachers in San Francisco who were either demoted or laid off were minorities.[24] It is not idle speculation to wonder how severely school budgets might have to be reduced and who might have to assume the brunt of cuts in future years when there will not be an available tax surplus.

Nor is the California public college and university system, often cited as the nation's best, spared from the reduced funding. It is feared that the state university and college system may have to reduce its budget by 10 percent, a 69 million cut.[25] Equally hard hit, if not more so, may be the community colleges, which receive 55 percent of their funding from property taxes. As a result of reduced budgets, 87 percent of last year's budgets, community colleges have suffered a 10 percent decline in enrollment, a loss of 125,000 students. In addition, community colleges have cut back the number of courses they offer by 6 percent and the number of classes offered by 13 percent. Full-time faculty members declined by 2.1 percent while part-time instructors declined by 22.9 percent.[26]

What will be the impact of these cuts and reductions on the access of black and other minority students at the colleges and universities in the system? There are predictions that tuition may be imposed and that open admissions may be restricted.[27] Such drastic steps could lead to decline in the enrollment of minority students. Again, if one uses the experiences of the City University of New York (CUNY) as a precedent, there is reason for alarm. For the imposition of tuition has been one factor in the reduction of minority enrollees, particularly minority males, in the CUNY system.[28]

Just as disturbing is how well the freeze on new hires and possible cutbacks in faculty size affect affirmative action programs at California colleges and universities. The experiences in recent years at Merritt College in Oakland, a case study in *The Case for Affirmative Action for Blacks in Higher Education*, offer a less than favorable future for affirmative action in an era of faculty retrenchment. The number of faculty members at Merritt declined from 188, in academic year 1972–1973, to 174 in the spring of 1976, with the number of black faculty members declining from 31 to 26.[29] Tensions are setting in throughout the system over the possible effects of cutbacks on affirmative action. According to one faculty member:

> . . . the social-justice attitudes of the most enlightened of our colleagues have been severely tested. Those of us who sought affirmative action now talk of 'them' getting 'our' jobs."[30]

These two trends, drops in minority enrollment and employment, pose serious threats to the attainment of equal educational and employment opportunity. Thus, a declining societal commitment to the public welfare now increases the possibilities of divisiveness among groups—the have and the have-nots—than any *unintended consequence* of the Great Society programs.

10

Affirmative Action: The *Bakke* and *Weber* Cases

Within the past two years the concept of affirmative action in education and in employment has weathered two more challenges before the Supreme Court, the first, in *Regents of the University of California* v. *Bakke* and the second in *United Steelworkers of America* v. *Weber.* At issue in *Bakke* was the legality of the special minority admissions program at the University of California-Davis Medical School whereby up to sixteen seats in the first year class were set aside for minority students.[1] At issue in *Weber* was the legality of a Kaiser Aluminum-United Steelworkers training program in which trainee slots were to be based upon a 50-50 ratio for blacks and whites.[2] These two cases are reflective of the changed, more hostile mood toward blacks. Central to this increasingly hostile attitude is the belief that government and society have been and are doing too much in behalf of blacks. As supporters of both Bakke and Weber would argue, racial discrimination in education and employment are largely vestiges of the past; thus, blacks should no longer be the recipients of "special favors" and "special treatment" from either government or society at large.

The *Bakke* and *Weber* cases, following upon *DeFunis* v. *Odegaard*, exemplify this new attitude. Although the Supreme Court's decisions in *Bakke* and *Weber* do differ and will be subjected to scrutiny by legal scholars, the threats to affirmative action programs continue. For the third time in three years, the Supreme Court will hear a case testing affirmative action. At issue in *Fullilove* v. *Kreps* is the constitutionality of a federal law, the Public Works Act of 1977,

63

which called for 10 percent of all government contracts funded under the law to go to minority contractors. The Supreme Court may also hear *Detroit Police Officers Association* v. *Young*, a suit brought by white police officers in Detroit against that city's affirmative action program for hiring and promoting black policemen. Thus, the assault against affirmative action continues.

Reactions to the *Bakke* Decision

On June 28, 1978, the Supreme Court issued its long awaited decision in the *Regents of the University of California* v. *Bakke* case. By a five-to-four margin, the Court, in upholding the decision of the California Supreme Court, struck down the special minority admissions program at the University of California-Davis Medical School and ordered that Allen Bakke be admitted. At the same time, and also by a five-to-four vote, the Supreme Court stated that colleges and universities could use race as a factor in determining who should be admitted.

Initial reactions to the *Bakke* decision varied: those who viewed the decision as harmful to blacks and other minorities; those who viewed the decision to admit Bakke with alarm, but who agreed with the Court's approving the use of race as a factor in the admission process; those who applauded the elimination of Davis' special minority admissions plan; and, those who praised the Court for eliminating the special minority admissions plan, but who decried the use of race as a factor in admissions.

Many black publications, leaders and educators, citing the overturning of the special minority admissions program at Davis, maintained that *Bakke* was a defeat, one potentially harmful for blacks. The *New York Amsterdam News* in a bold headline announced "Bakke: We Lose!"[3] The *Pittsburgh Courier's* lead story announced "Top Court Backs Bakke" and its major editorial was entitled "A Racist Decision."[4] The initial comments and reactions of many blacks showed equal dismay. Congressman Ronald Dellums called the decision "racist" and a "barrier to the assurance of racial justice in this country."[5] Jesse Jackson called the decision a "devastating blow," one which "will harden the hearts of those who resist justice and equality for black people."[6] Dr. Kenneth Tollett, Director of the Institute for the Study of Educational Policy at Howard University, called the decision "a hammer in the solar plexus."[7] Harvard professor Alvin Poussaint saw the decision as having a "heavy, negative effect on affirmative action programs."[8]

The initial responses of other blacks were more optimistic, stressing that the Supreme Court did hold that race could be a factor in admissions. Vernon Jordan argued that the decision "was no defeat, but it was no victory either."[9] Benjamin Hooks maintained "Allan Bakke did win a battle but not a war."[10] M. Carl Holman, President of the National Urban Coalition, stressed that other affirmative action programs, "more flexible" than Davis' were still allowed.[11]

Washington Post columnist William Raspberry described the decision as ambiguous, but added "I, for one, welcome the ambiguity."[12]

Supporters of Allan Bakke expressed their delight with the Supreme Court's decision. Sam Rabinove, legal director of the American Jewish Committee and Howard M. Squadron, President of the American Jewish Congress, expressed their pleasure at the overturning of the special minority admissions program at Davis.[13] Nathan Glazer termed the Supreme Court's action "the kind of human behavior any commonsensical human being would believe in."[14] Thomas Sowell praised both the "resolve and courage" of Bakke and "the carefully reasoned decision" of Justice Powell.[15] Less guarded expressions of praise came from Marco DeFunis who four years earlier had challenged the special minority admissions program at the University of Washington. While expressing his pleasure at the overturning of the "fixed-quota admissions policy," DeFunis was "bothered by the argument that academic freedom allows race to be considered."[16]

The *Bakke* case has been and will continue to be the focus of legal commentary and lay analysis in the future. Much of this commentary has centered and will center around the meaning and the impact of the decision. Opponents of special minority admissions programs, such as Yale Law Professor Robert H. Bork and University of Chicago Law Professor Philip B. Kurland, contend that *Bakke* will lead to further law suits.[17] Other critics take a more scathing view of the decisions. George Will writes: "the *Bakke* decision will leave unscathed an array of programs by which the government encourages or compels public and private institutions to consider ethnic quantities more, and individual qualities less, when conferring benefits."[18] The critics of special minority admissions programs are undecided as to whether or not *Bakke* is a landmark. What does strike them as a potential landmark are the opinions of Justices Brennan, White, and Marshall. According to Allan P. Sindler, these justices "developed and subscribed to a constitutional justification of pro-minority racial preferences and reverse discrimination that would transform the meaning of equal protection and equal opportunity."[19]

While critics of special minority admissions plans and affirmative action plans offer scathing attacks upon the opinion of the Brennan bloc, especially the opinion of Justice Marshall, the supporters of affirmative action have been favorable.[20] Marshall's opinion has been reprinted and cited for what it accurately states: the current status and situation of blacks in the United States.[21] Moreover, as is the theme of a recent issue of the *Harvard Civil Rights-Civil Liberties Law Review*, there is still in the aftermath of *Bakke* a very strong need for affirmative action programs to "redress the social history of racism."[22]

Note: see Appendix for Justice Marshall's dissent.

The Effects of *Bakke*: A Preliminary Assessment

It has been argued that future litigation will determine the effects of *Bakke*. Yet, *Bakke* has already been cited as legal precedent. In *Uzell* v. *Friday,* the United States Fourth Circuit Court of Appeals cited the decision in *Bakke* in striking down a student body regulation at the University of North Carolina providing at least two seats for minority students in the student honor court.[23] Moreover, the Court's decision in *Bakke* has been cited in at least two cases involving the Public Works Act of 1977. Under the provisions of the act, ten percent of the four billion dollars allocated for public work construction was to be set aside for minority contractors. Contractors' associations across the country filed suit contending that the law involved quotas, although *only* ten percent of the monies were to be set aside. In *Associated General Contractors of California* v. *Secretary of Commerce,* a district court in California held "in the wake of *Bakke* . . . the 10 percent race quota was not a constitutionally acceptable means of promoting the Congress' legitimate interest in promoting employment in the construction industry among minority group members."[24] However, in *Fullilove* v. *Kreps,* currently before the Supreme Court, the Second Circuit Court of Appeals upheld the Public Works Act. Citing *Bakke,* the Court held that the setting of contracts for minorities was a justifiable remedy in overcoming past racial discrimination in employment.[25]

As a result of the Supreme Court's decision in *Bakke,* numerous graduate and professional schools have revised their admissions programs and procedures. The Stanford University Medical Center, the University of Pennsylvania Law School, the New York University Law School, the Rutgers-Newark Law School and the University of Illinois Law School, the UCLA Law School, and the University of California-Davis Medical School have disbanded their special minority admissions programs. In their place, they have instituted new policies which consider race and ethnicity as a factor or which allow disadvantaged whites to be considered for admission under expanded slots for the disadvantaged.[26]

The National Conference of Black Lawyers (NCBL) has praised the new admissions program for the disadvantaged at the Rutgers-Newark Law School as a "positive solution" inasmuch as 30 percent of the seats will be reserved for disadvantaged students.[27] However, black leaders, black lawyers, and black students are somewhat fearful of the impact of those new admissions procedures upon minority enrollments. Vernon Jordan has stated that the broadening definition of the term "economically disadvantaged" and wider application of "minority" threaten to dilute the special programs and opportunities originally designed in behalf of blacks.[28] Benjamin Hooks, in citing the disbanding of special minority admissions programs, has argued that the *Bakke* decision has led "a lot of so-called liberal schools in this country to abandon the affirmative action concept."[29] Wade J. Henderson, Executive Director of the Council on

Legal Education Opportunity (CLEO), has argued that *Bakke* has had "a chilling impact" on the application of minority group students to professional schools.[30] Henderson's views have been echoed by Victor Goode of the NCBL and University of Pennsylvania law professor Ralph Smith who have expressed alarm and dismay at the dismantling of special minority admissions programs and the impact of such dismantlings upon the enrollment of black students.[31] Black students at these respective campuses question the continued commitment of professional and graduate schools to enrolling black and other minority students.[32]

Despite recent assertions by professional associations that the *Bakke* decision has had "virtually no effect" and "little impact" upon the admissions of minority students,[33] preliminary data indicate that the controversy surrounding the *Bakke* case did have a chilling effect upon the enrolling of black students into professional schools. While the total enrollment in medical schools increased by nearly four hundred students for the class admitted in the Fall of 1978, the number of black first year students declined.[34] In addition, the percentage of blacks in medical schools continued to drop. From the high of 7.5 percent in 1974, black enrollment declined to 6.7 percent in 1977 and to 6.4 percent in 1978.[35] And while the overall minority student enrollment is expected to be around 9 percent for the fall of 1979, black enrollment is estimated to be 6.1 percent, a further decline.[36] This decline in enrollment of black and other minority students in graduate and professional schools is more glaring when specific programs are examined. At Stanford University the number of minority students enrolled in the graduate and professional programs declined from 533, in academic year 1973-74, to 388 in academic year 1978-79. At the University of Pennsylvania Law School, one of those schools which disbanded its special minority admissions programs, the number of black first year students declined from 47 in 1976-77 to 28 in the fall of 1979.[37]

Many graduate and professional schools have disbanded their special minority admissions programs and have implemented new policies designed to diversify their student bodies in terms of "economically disadvantaged" students. The efforts of some schools have been criticized in a recent report issued by the Anti-Defamation League of B'nai B'rith. Surveying the admissions policies and procedures of most law, medical, and dental schools, the report claimed that sixteen schools continued to have "facially discriminatory admissions procedures based on ethnic/racial classifications." Twenty other schools were allegedly using procedures and practices "visibly suspect with respect to the ethnic/racial classifications made illegal by *Bakke*."[38] While not specifically naming schools, several of those cited are among those disbanding special minority admissions programs in favor of new programs. One law school, obviously Rutgers-Newark, was chided for its 30 percent Minority Student Program, including economically and educationally disadvantaged whites. According to B'nai B'rith, this plan is a quota and gives preferential treatment to black applicants, "no matter how wealthy or well-educated."[39] Such comments are part of how perceptions of black progress can impede the continuance of affirmative action programs.

The new program at Rutgers-Newark was only one of those allegedly in violation of *Bakke*. Another program considered to be in violation of *Bakke* is the new admissions procedures at the UCLA Law School. Sixty percent of the admissions were to be based on test scores and grades, while the other forty percent were to be based upon academic potential, career goals, work experience and race. Yet, the B'nai B'rith report attacks this program, again one benefitting both black and white applicants, as a "two-track system."[40] The procedures at Rutgers-Newark and UCLA have been reluctantly accepted by black and other minority students as compromises.[41] Yet, the response of B'nai B'rith to these new procedures has been to continue to stress *meritocracy* rather than *diversity*. This hostility to programs which encourage diversity for both educationally and economically disadvantaged blacks *and* whites leads one to question how far the opinions in *Bakke* will be extended in criticizing efforts to increase minority enrollments in graduate and professional schools.

Nor are black professional schools spared from this scrutiny. In an analysis of the impact of *Bakke* upon black colleges, Derrick Bell contended as a result of the decision "it is far from clear that black colleges can give absolute preferences to black applicants, despite their historical mission of educating blacks and the increased efficiency and dedication they are bringing to the task."[42] Bell's analysis is not an overstatement. This is clearly the case at the North Carolina Central University Law School, now 45 percent white, and where administrators are trying hard to retain a "substantial black enrollment."[43] One of the schools described in the B'nai B'rith report as a "special situation," nevertheless a school whose admissions procedures are allegedly "suspect," sounds very much like the Howard University School of Dentistry.[44] Although the Howard University School of Dentistry has traditionally had a relatively high number of white students, its admissions procedures are considered by B'nai B'rith to be "suspect," because it *still* offers a "program in which minority students form the majority and for whom the program is focused."[45]

A preliminary assessment of the impact of the *Bakke* decision reveals more negative signals than positive trends. Special minority admissions programs have been eliminated by many graduate and professional schools in the wake of *Bakke*. Their replacements, programs in which race does play a factor on the admissions process, have been criticized for not being in compliance with *Bakke*. Moreover, *Bakke* does pose a threat to the graduate and professional programs at black universities. These schools, with a far better record in admitting white students, find themselves in a dilemma in trying to fulfill their historic mission in educating blacks. To say that *Bakke* has had virtually no effect and little impact is far too optimistic an assessment.

The *Weber* Decision

On June 29, 1979, a year and a day after its decision in *Bakke,* the Supreme Court issued its decision in *United Steelworkers* v. *Weber.* By a 5 to 2 vote the Court reversed the decisions of a Louisiana district court and the Fifth Circuit Court of Appeals and upheld the training program developed by Kaiser Aluminum and the United Steelworkers that reserved 50 percent of the training slots for black workers. In the majority opinion, Justice Brennan stated that Title VII of the 1964 Civil Rights Act "does not prohibit such race-conscious affirmative action plans" as the voluntary plan developed by Kaiser Aluminum and United Steelworkers. Briefly reviewing the legislative history of Title VII, Brennan wrote that the Kaiser-United Steelworkers plan was within the spirit of Title VII, as can be determined from the framers' intent.[46]

Conservative and neo-conservative critics of affirmative action programs such as George F. Will, James J. Kilpatrick, Patrick Buchanan, William Buckley and Carl Cohen have assailed the majority opinion, particularly Justice Brennan's discussion of the legislative history of Title VII.[47] Repeatedly citing Justice Rehnquist's dissent, they stress that the intent of the law was to end discrimination in employment. With the same allegiance to "color blind" and "racially neutral" practices and procedures that they expressed during the debate over *Bakke,* these critics continue to forget the persistence of discrimination encountered by blacks and other minorities. While bemoaning the alleged "reverse discrimination" faced by Allan Bakke, they were and are unmindful of the *real* discrimination encountered by blacks and women that led to the civil rights settlement against the American Telephone and Telegraph Company. While bemoaning the plight of Brian Weber, these very same critics are either unmindful to or forgetful of promotions denied to black workers. Detroit Edison has agreed to pay $4.25 million in back pay to black workers denied promotions because of race and another $850,000 to blacks whose job applications were turned down.[48] While the experiences of Allan Bakke and Brian Weber can arouse the ire of journalists who denounce affirmative action programs as violation of their individual rights, these commentators do not make mention of how the rights of literally hundreds of blacks are violated and how blacks as individuals and blacks as a group are continually denied equal opportunity.

Black columnists, leaders, and spokespersons have welcomed the Supreme Court's decision in *Weber.* Columnist William Raspberry welcomed the decision as "the right spirit." In the same manner, columnist Carl Rowan praised the majority opinion for unmasking the "true congressional intent" behind Title VII—to aid blacks, not white males.[49] Joseph E. Lowery, president of Southern Christian Leadership Conference (SCLC), stated that the decision in *Weber* provided "a green light now for employers and labor unions to accelerate their programs to train and upgrade minorities." Both Benjamin Hooks and Vernon

Jordan expressed elation, coupled with caution, at the decision. While praising the decision, Hooks stated that blacks should not have had to be grateful "for something which justice dictates we should never have had to ask for." Vernon Jordan, in assessing both the unemployment rates for blacks and the support given to Weber, has argued that *Weber* was "just the beginning, not the end of the fight for affirmative action."[50]

While Weber is indeed a victory for supporters of affirmative action in employment, the assault against affirmative action continues. Aside from future court challenges to the constitutionality of minority set aside contracts or to other affirmative action programs in employment, there is the very real threat posed by congressional legislation to affirmative action programs in education and in employment. Over the past two years the House has passed amendments to congressional bills prohibiting the use of federal funds to enforce any "ratio, quota, or other numerical requirement related to race or sex in hiring, promotions, and university admissions."[51] With a more conservative Congress, this type of legislation stands a better chance of passage as witnessed by the amending of the bill creating the Department of Education. Moreover, in the wake of *Weber,* a bill has been introduced into the Senate to amend Title VII of the 1964 Civil Rights Act.[52] Thus *Weber,* while providing a further clarification and endorsement of the concept of affirmative action as a remedy to ensure equal opportunity, has not settled the continuing controversy surrounding affirmative action programs.

Afterword

The arguments analyzed in the preceding chapters do indicate rather strongly that there is a changed mood in the country toward blacks, other minorities and the poor. The national spirit and will that led to the enactment of the Great Society and the War on Poverty programs have been usurped by the growing hostility to social welfare programs. Detractors and critics of these programs point to their alleged failure and castigate the continuance of these social welfare efforts. However, these efforts have not been and are not "failures." They have brought benefits and relief, both immediate and long term, to those who are the beneficiaries. Programs such as food stamps, public assistance, and increased social security have provided immediate relief to the most disadvantaged Americans. Moreover, the oft-criticized compensatory education programs such as Head Start and Title I have been found to be far more successful than their critics allege. These programs have helped to *establish* and to *nourish* those characteristics and habits essential to educational success. Thus, these programs are not indicative of the failure of the strategy of "throwing money at problems." Rather, their successes reveal rather poignantly that "money can make a difference."

Similarly, benefits have resulted from programs and strategies designed to insure equal educational and economic opportunities for blacks, other minorities, and the poor. While busing may or may not have contributed to the phenomenon of white flight, it has certainly not led to declining educational achievement. In more cases than not, the imposition of busing has led to increased educational achievement and attainment by black students. At the same time, busing has not led to a decline in the achievement scores of white students. Thus, as this monograph repeatedly points out, strategies to improve equal educational and

71

economic opportunities for blacks, other minorities, and the poor are vital tools in the effort to bring about a fairer and more equitable society.

How then does one *change* or *redirect* the present mood and attitude of hostility toward these efforts? Frankly, there is no instant answer or panacea. Attitudes against governmental and societal efforts designed to help the disadvantaged have hardened. Thus, appeals to the American populace in behalf of attempts to reduce economic inequities and to redress both past discrimination and the present effects of such discrimination often fall on deaf ears. While it is socially and politically fashionable to call for cutbacks in social welfare programs, such calls should not deter those—individuals and groups—who still "keep the faith" and believe strongly in the efficacy of governmental and societal efforts at reform. One possible strategy may be for blacks, other minorities and the poor to make use of the tactics employed in the 1960s. Perhaps marches and demonstrations may once again focus attention and concern upon their plight and condition relative to the larger society. Just as these activities were instrumental in spawning government and societal concern in the 1960s, renewal of marches and demonstrations hopefully will rekindle commitments to economic equity and social justice. Moreover, in terms of present strategy and future tactics, supporters and proponents of social welfare programs need to be ever vigilant in their defense of these programs. However, the defense should not rest solely on calls for the continued existence of social welfare programs in the face of criticism. Supporters of these programs must make known to the public the real and lasting gains that these efforts have had and will have to individuals and in turn to the larger society. Instead of cutbacks in funding, supporters must argue for continued, and in some cases, expanded funding for these efforts. It is not enough to analyze favorably the work to date of programs such as Head Start. Efforts and strategies must be made to expand further the scope and thrust of such programs.

As the nation witnesses the beginning of the 1980 presidential campaign, it is hoped that the respective candidates for nomination do not lose sight of the current *plight* of the disadvantaged. And as the nation enters the 1980s may there be a reaffirmation of both the national spirit and will to achieve the "Great Society."

Appendix
Notes
Index

Appendix

No. 76-811

Regents of the University of California, Petitioner, *v.* Allan Bakke.	On Writ of Certiorari to the Supreme Court of California

[June 28, 1978]

MR. JUSTICE MARSHALL.

I agree with the judgment of the Court only insofar as it permits a university to consider the race of an applicant in making admissions decisions. I do not agree that petitioner's admissions program violates the Constitution. For it must be remembered that, during most of the past 200 years, the Constitution as interpreted by this Court did not prohibit the most ingenious and pervasive forms of discrimination against the Negro. Now, when a State acts to remedy the effects of that legacy of discrimination, I cannot believe that this same Constitution stands as a barrier.

I

A

Three hundred and fifty years ago, the Negro was dragged to this country in chains to be sold into slavery. Uprooted from his homeland and thrust into bondage for forced labor, the slave was deprived of all legal rights. It was unlawful to teach him to read; he could be sold away from his family and friends at the whim of his master; and killing or maiming him was not a crime. The system of slavery brutalized and dehumanized both master and slave.[1]

The denial of human rights was etched into the American colonies' first attempts at establishing self-government. When the colonists determined to seek their independence from England, they drafted a unique document cataloguing their grievances against the King and proclaiming as "self-evident" that "all men are created equal" and are endowed "with certain unalienable Rights," including those to "Life, Liberty and the pursuit of Happiness." The self-evident truths and the unalienable rights were intended,

---

[1]The history recounted here is perhaps too well known to require documentation. But I must acknowledge the authorities on which I rely in retelling it. J. H. Franklin, From Slavery to Freedom, (4th ed. 1974) (hereinafter Franklin); R. Kluger, Simple Justice (1975) (hereinafter Kluger); C. V. Woodward, The Strange Career of Jim Crow (3rd ed. 1974) (hereinafter Woodward).

however, to apply only to white men. An earlier draft of the Declaration of Independence, submitted by Thomas Jefferson to the Continental Congress, had included among the charges against the King that

> "[h]e has waged cruel war against human nature itself, violating its most sacred rights of life and liberty in the persons of a distant people who never offended him, captivating and carrying them into slavery in another hemisphere, or to incur miserable death in their transportation thither." Franklin 88.

The Southern delegation insisted that the charge be deleted; the colonists themselves were implicated in the slave trade, and inclusion of this claim might have made it more difficult to justify the continuation of slavery once the ties to England were severed. Thus, even as the colonists embarked on a course to secure their own freedom and equality, they ensured perpetuation of the system that deprived a whole race of those rights.

The implicit protection of slavery embodied in the Declaration of Independence was made explicit in the Constitution, which treated a slave as being equivalent to three-fifths of a person for purposes of appointing representatives and taxes among the States. Art, I. §2. The Constitution also contained a clause ensuring that the "migration or importation" of slaves into the existing States would be legal until at least 1808. Art. I. §9, and a fugitive slave clause requiring that when a slave escaped to another State, he must be returned on the claim of the master. Art. IV. §2. In their declaration of the principles that were to provide the cornerstone of the new Nation, therefore, the Framers made it plain that "we the people," for whose protection the Constitution was designed, did not include those whose skins were the wrong color. As Professor John Hope Franklin has observed, Americans "proudly accepted the challenge and responsibility of their new political freedom by establishing the machinery and safeguards that insured the continued enslavement of blacks." Franklin 100.

The individual States likewise established the machinery to protect the system of slavery through the promulgation of the Slave Codes, which were designed primarily to defend the property interest of the owner in his slave. The position of the Negro slave as mere property was confirmed by this Court in *Dred Scott* v. *Sandford,* 19 How. 393 (1857), holding that the Missouri Compromise—which prohibited slavery in the portion of the Louisiana Purchase Territory north of Missouri—was unconstitutional because it deprived slave owners of their property without due process. The Court declared that under the Constitution a slave was property, and "[t]he right to traffic in it, like an ordinary article of merchandise and property, was guarantied to the citizens of the United States. ..." *Id.,* at 451. The Court further concluded that Negroes were not intended to be included as citizens under the Constitution but were "regarded as beings of an inferior order ... altogether unfit to associate with the white race, either in social or political relations; and so far inferior, that they had no rights which the white man was bound to respect. ..." *Id.,* at 407.

B

The status of the Negro as property was officially erased by his emancipation at the end of the Civil War. But the long awaited emancipation, while freeing the Negro from slavery, did not bring him citizenship or equality in any meaningful way. Slavery was replaced by a system of "laws which imposed upon the colored race onerous disabilities and burdens, and curtailed their rights in the pursuit of life, liberty, and property to such an extent that their freedom was of little value." *Slaughter-House Cases,* 16 Wall. 36. 70 (1873). Despite the passage of the Thirteenth, Fourteenth, and Fifteenth Amendments, the Negro was systematically denied the rights those amendments were suppose to secure. The combined actions and inactions of the State and Federal Government maintained Negroes in a position of legal inferiority for another century after the Civil War.

The Southern States took the first steps to re-enslave the Negroes. Immediately following the end of the Civil War, many of the provisional legislatures passed Black Codes, similar to the Slave Codes, which, among other things, limited the rights of Negroes to own or rent property and permitted imprisonment for breach of employment contracts. Over the next several decades the South managed to disenfranchise the Negroes in spite of the Fifteenth Amendment by various techniques, including poll taxes, deliberately complicated balloting process, property and literacy qualifications, and finally the white primary.

Congress responded to the legal disabilities being imposed in the Southern States by passing the Reconstruction Acts and the Civil Rights Acts. Congress also responded to the needs of the Negroes at the end of the Civil War by establishing the Bureau of Refugees, Freedmen, and Abandoned Lands, better known as the Freedmen's Bureau, to supply food, hospitals, land and education to the newly freed slaves. Thus for a time it seemed as if the Negro might be protected from the continued denial of his civil rights and might be relieved of the disabilities that prevented him from taking his place as a free and equal citizen.

That time, however, was short-lived. Reconstruction came to a close, and, with the assistance of this Court, the Negro was rapidly stripped of his new civil rights. In the words of C. Vann Woodward: "By narrow and ingenious interpretation [the Supreme Court's] decisions over a period of years had whittled away a great part of the authority presumably given the government for protection of civil rights." Woodward 139.

The Court began by interpreting the Civil War Amendments in a manner that sharply curtailed their substantive protections. See, *e.g., Slaughter-House Cases. supra; United States* v. *Reese,* 92 U.S. 214 (1876); *United States* v. *Cruikshank,* 92 U.S. 542 (1876). Then in the notorious *Civil Rights Cases,* 109 U.S. 3 (1883), the Court strangled Congress' efforts to use its power to promote racial equality. In those cases the Court invalidated sections of the Civil Rights Act of 1875 that made it a crimes to deny equal access to "inns, public conveyances. ... theatres, and other places of public amusement." According to the Court, the Fourteenth Amendment gave Congress the power to prescribe only discriminatory action by the State. The Court ruled that the Negroes who were excluded from public places suffered only an invasion of their social rights at the hands of private individuals, and Congress had no power to remedy that. *Id.,* at 24-25. "When a man has emerged from slavery, and by the aid of beneficient legislation has shaken off the inseparable concomitants of that state," the Court concluded, "there must be some stage in the progress of his elevation when he takes the rank of a mere citizen, and ceases to be the special favorite of the laws. ..." *Id.,* at 25. As Justice Harlan noted in dissent, however, the Civil War Amendments and Civil Rights Acts did not make the Negroes the "special favorite" of the laws but instead "sought to accomplish in reference to that race ... what had already been done in every State of the Union for the White race—to secure and protect rights belonging to them as freemen and citizens; nothing more." *Id.,* at 61.

The Court's ultimate blow to the Civil War Amendments and to the equality of Negroes came in *Plessy* v. *Ferguson,* 163 U.S. 537 (1896). In upholding a Louisiana law that required railway companies to provide "equal but separate" accommodations for whites and Negroes, the Court held that the Fourteenth Amendment was not intended "to abolish distinctions based upon color, or to enforce social, as distinguished from political equality, or a commingling of the two races upon terms unsatisfactory to either." *Id.,* at 544. Ignoring totally the realities of the positions of the two races, the Court remarked:

"We consider the underlying fallacy of the plaintiff's argument to consist in the assumption that the enforced separation of the two races stamps the colored race with a badge of inferiority. If this be so, it is not by reason of anything found in the act but solely because the colored race chooses to put that construction upon it." *Id.*, at 551.

Mr. Justice Harlan's dissenting opinion recognized the bankruptcy of the Court's reasoning. He noted that the "real meaning" of the legislation was "that colored citizens are so inferior and degraded that they cannot be allowed to sit in public coaches occupied by white citizens." *Id.*, at 560. He expressed his fear that if like laws were enacted in other States, "the effect would be in the highest degree mischevious." *Id.*, at 503. Although slavery would have disappeared, the States would retain the power "to interfere with the full enjoyment of the blessings of freedom; to regulate civil rights, common to all citizens, upon the basis of race; and to place in a condition of legal inferiority a large body of American citizens. ..." *Id.*, at 563.

The fears of Mr. Justice Harlan were soon to be realized. In the wake of *Plessy,* many States expanded their Jim Crow laws, which had up until that time been limited primarily to passenger trains and schools. The segregation of the races was extended to residential areas, parks, hospitals, theaters, waiting rooms and bathrooms. There were even statutes and ordinances which authorized separate phone booths for Negroes and whites, which required that textbooks used by children of one race be kept separate from those used by the other, and which required that Negro and white prostitutes be kept in separate districts. In 1898, after *Plessy,* the Charlestown News and Courier printed a parody of Jim Crow laws:

"If there must be Jim Crow cars on the railroads, there should be Jim Crow cars on the street railways. Also on all passenger boats. ... If there are to be Jim Crow cars, moreover, there should be Jim Crow waiting saloons at all stations, and Jim Crow eating houses. ... There should be Jim Crow sections of the jury box, and a separate Jim Crow dock and witness stand in every court—and a Jim Crow Bible for colored witnesses to kiss." Woodward 68.

The irony is that before many years had passed, with the exception of the Jim Crow witness stand, "all the improbable applications of the principle suggested by the editor in derision had been put into practice—down to and including the Jim Crow Bible." Woodward 69.

Nor were the laws restricting the rights of Negroes limited solely to the Southern States. In many of the Northern States, the Negro was denied the right to vote, prevented from serving on juries and excluded from theaters, restaurants, hotels, and inns. Under President Wilson, the Federal Government began to require segregation in Government buildings; desks of Negro employees were curtained off; separate bathrooms and separate tables in the cafeterias were provided; and even the galleries of the Congress were segregated. When his segregationist policies were attacked, President Wilson responded that segregation was "not humiliating but a benefit" and that he was "rendering [the Negroes] more safe in their possession of office and less likely to be discriminated against." Kluger 91.

The enforced segregation of the races continued into the middle of the 20th century. In both World Wars, Negroes were for the most part confined to separate military units; it was not until 1948 that an end to segregation in the military was ordered by President Truman. And the history of the exclusion of Negro children from white public schools is too well known and recent to require repeating here. That Negroes were deliberately excluded from public graduate and professional schools—and thereby denied the opportunity to become doctors, lawyers, engineers, and the like—is also well established. It is of course true that some of the Jim Crow laws (which the decisions of this Court had helped to foster) were struck down by this Court in a series of decisions leading up to *Brown* v. *Board of Education of Topeka*, 347 U.S. 483 (1954). See, *e.g., Morgan* v. *Virginia*, 328 U.S. 373 (1946); *Sweatt* v. *Painter*, 339 U.S. 629 (1950); *McLaurin* v. *Oklahoma State Regents*, 339 U.S. 637 (1950). Those decisions, however, did not automatically end segregation, nor did they move Negroes from a position of legal inferiority to one of equality. The legacy of years of slavery and of years of second-class citizenship in the wake of emancipation could not be so easily eliminated.

II

The position of the Negro today in America is the tragic but inevitable consequence of centuries of unequal treatment. Measured by any benchmark of comfort or achievement, meaningful equality remains a distant dream for the Negro.

A Negro child today has a life expectancy which is shorter by more than five years than that of a white child.[2] The Negro child's mother is over three times more likely to die of complications in childbirth,[3] and the infant mortality rate for Negroes is nearly twice that for whites.[4] The median income of the Negro family is only 60% that of the median of a white family,[5] and the percentage of Negroes who live in families with incomes below the poverty line is nearly four times greater than that of whites.[6]

When the Negro child reaches working age, he finds that America offers him significantly less than it offers his white counterpart. For Negro adults, the unemployment rate is twice that of whites,[7] and the unemployment rate for Negro teenagers is nearly three times that of white teenagers.[8] A Negro male who completes four years of college can expect a median annual income of merely $110 more than a white male who has only a high school diploma.[9] Although Negroes represent 11.5% of the population,[10] they are only 1.2% of the lawyers and judges, 2% of the physicians, 2.3% of the dentists, 1.1% of the engineers and 2.6% of the college and university professors.[11]

The relationship between those figures and the history of unequal treatment afforded to the Negro cannot be denied. At every point from birth to death the impact of the past is reflected in the still disfavored position of the Negro.

In the light of the sorry history of discrimination and its devastating impact on the lives of Negroes, bringing the Negro into the mainstream of American life should be a state interest of the highest order. To fail to do so is to ensure that America will forever remain a divided society.

---

[2]U.S. Dept. of Commerce, Bureau of the Census, Statistical Abstract of the United States 65 (1977) (table 94).
[3]*Id.,* at 70 (table 102).
[4]*Ibid.*
[5]U.S. Dept. of Commerce, Bureau of the Census, Current Population Reports, Series P-60. No. 107, at 7 (1977) (table 1).
[6]*Id.,* at 20 (table 14).
[7]U.S. Dept. of Labor, Bureau of Labor Statistics, Employment and Earnings, January 1978, at 170 (table 44).
[8]*Ibid.*
[9]U.S. Dept. of Commerce, Bureau of the Census. Current Population Reports, Series P-60. No. 105, at 198 (1977) (table 47).
[10]U.S. Dept. of Commerce, Bureau of the Census, Statistical Abstract of the United States 25 (table 24).
[11]*Id.,* at 407–408 (table 662) (based on 1970 census).

III

I do not believe that the Fourteenth Amendment requires us to accept that fate. Neither its history nor our past cases lend any support to the conclusion that a University may not remedy the cumulative effects of society's discrimination by giving consideration to race in an effort to increase the number and percentage of Negro doctors.

A

This Court long ago remarked that

> "in any fair and just construction of any section or phrase of these [Civil War] amendments, it is necessary to look to the purpose which we have said was the pervading spirt of them all, the evil which they were designed to remedy. ..." *Slaughter-House Cases,* 16 Wall., at 72.

It is plain that the Fourteenth Amendment was not intended to prohibit measures designed to remedy the effects of the Nation's past treatment of Negroes. The Congress that passed the Fourteenth Amendment is the same Congress that passed the 1866 Freedmen's Bureau Act, an act that provided many of its benefits only to Negroes. Act of July 16, 1866, ch. 200, 14 Stat. 173; see p. 4. *supra.* Although the Freedmen's Bureau legislation provided aid for, refugees, thereby including white persons within some of the relief measures. 14 Stat., at 174; see also Act of Mar. 3, 1865. ch. 90. 13 Stat. 507, the bill was regarded, to the dismay of many Congressmen, as "solely and entirely for the freedmen, and to the exclusion of all other persons...." Cong. Globe, 39th Cong., 1st Sess. 544 (1866) (remarks of Rep. Taylor). See also *id.,* at 634–635 (remarks of Rep. Chanler). Indeed, the bill was bitterly opposed on the ground that it "undertakes to make the negro in some respects ... superior ... and gives them favors that the poor white boy in the North cannot get." *Id.,* at 401, (remarks of Sen. McDougall). See also *id.,* at 319 (remarks of Sen. Hendricks); *id.,* at 362 (remarks of Sen. Saulsbury); *id.,* at 397 (remarks of Sen. Willey); *id.,* at 544 (remarks of Rep. Taylor). The bill's supporters defended it—not by rebutting the claim of special treatment—but by pointing to the need for such treatment:

> "The very discrimination it makes between 'destitute and suffering' negroes and destitute and suffering white paupers, proceeds upon the distinction that, in the omitted case, civil rights and immunities are already sufficiently protected by the possession of political power, the absence of which in the case provided for necessitates governmental protection." *Id.,* at 75 (remarks of Rep. Phelps).

Despite the objection to the special treatment the bill would provide for Negroes, it was passed by Congress. *Id.,* at 421 688. President Johnson vetoed this bill and also a subsequent bill that contained some modifications; one of his principal objections to both bills was that they gave special benefits to Negroes. VIII Messages and Papers of the Presidents 3596, 3599, 3620, 3623 (1866). Rejecting the concerns of the President and the bill's opponents, Congress overrode the President's second veto. Cong. Globe, at 3842, 3850.

Since the Congress that considered and rejected the objections to the 1866 Freedman's Bureau Act concerning special relief to Negroes also proposed the Fourteenth Amendment, it is inconceivable that the Fourteenth Amendment was intended to prohibit all race-conscious relief measures. It "would be a distortion of the policy manifested in that amendment, which was adopted to prevent state legislation designed to perpetuate discrimination on the basis of race or color," *Railway Mail Association* v. *Corsi,* 326 U.S. 88.94 (1945), to hold that it barred state action to remedy the effects of that discrimination.

Such a result would pervert the intent of the framers by substituting abstract equality for the genuine equality the amendment was intended to achieve.

B

As has been demonstrated in our joint opinion, this Court's past cases establish the constitutionality of race-conscious remedial measures. Beginning with the school desegregation cases, we recognized that even absent a judicial or legislative finding of constitutional violation, a school board constitutionally could consider the race of students in making school assignment decisions. See *Swann* v. *Charlotte-Mecklenberg Board of Education*, 402 U.S. 1, 16 (1971); *McDaniel* v. *Barresi*, 402 U.S. 39.41 (1971). We noted, moreover, that a

> "flat prohibition against assignment of students for the purpose of creating a racial balance must inevitably conflict with the duty of school authorities to disestablish dual school systems. As we have held in *Swann*, the Constitution does not compel any particular degree of racial balance or mixing, but when past and continuing constitutional violations are found, some ratios are likely to be useful as starting points in shaping a remedy. An absolute prohibition against use of such a device—even as a starting point—contravenes the implicit command of *Green* v. *County School Board*, 391 U.S. 430 (1968), that all reasonable methods be available to formulate an effective remedy." *Board of Education* v. *Swann*, 402 U.S. 43, 46 (1971).

As we have observed, "[a]ny other approach would freeze the status quo that is the very target of all desegregation processes." *McDaniel* v. *Barresi, supra*, at 41.

Only last Term, in *United Jewish Organizations* v. *Carey* 430 U.S. 144 (1977), we upheld a New York reapportionment plan that was deliberately drawn on the basis of race to enhance the electoral power of Negroes and Puerto Ricans; the plan had the effect of diluting the electoral strength of the Hasidic Jewish Community. We were willing in *UJO* to sanction the remedial use of a racial classification even though it disadvantaged otherwise "innocent" individuals. In another case last Term, *Califano* v. *Webster*, 430 U.S. 313 (1977), the Court upheld a provision in the Social Security laws that discriminated against men because its purpose was " 'the permissible one of redressing our society's long standing disparate treatment of women.' " *Id.*, at 317, quoting *Califano* v. *Goldfarb*, 430 U.S. 199, 209 n. 8 (1977) (plurality opinion). We thus recognized the permissibility of remedying past societal discrimination through the use of otherwise disfavored classifications.

Nothing in those cases suggests that a university cannot similarly act to remedy past discrimination.[12] It is true that in both *UJO* and *Webster* the use of the disfavored classification was predicated on legislative or administrative action, but in neither case had those bodies made findings that there had been constitutional violations or that the specific individuals to be benefited had actually been the victims of discrimination. Rather, the classification in each of those cases was based on a determination that the group was in need of the remedy because of some type of past discrimination. There is thus ample support for the conclusion that a university can employ race-conscious measures to remedy past societal discrimination, without the need for a finding that those benefited were actually victims of that discrimination.

---

[12]Indeed, the action of the University finds support in the regulations promulgated under Title VI by the Department of Health, Education, and Welfare and approved by the President, which authorize a federally funded institution to take affirmative steps to overcome past discrimination against groups even where the institution was not guilty of prior discrimination. 45 CFR 80.3 (b) (6) (ii) (1977).

IV

While I applaud the judgment of the Court that a university may consider race in its admissions process, it is more than a little ironic that, after several hundred years of class-based discrimination against Negroes, the Court is unwilling to hold that a class-based remedy for that discrimination is permissible. In declining to so hold, today's judgment ignores the fact that for several hundred years Negroes have been discriminated against, not as individuals, but rather solely because of the color of their skins. It is unnecessary in 20th century America to have individual Negroes demonstrate that they have been victims of racial discrimination; the racism of our society has been so pervasive that none, regardless of wealth or position, has managed to escape its impact. The experience of Negroes in America has been different in kind, not just in degree, from that of other ethnic groups. It is not merely the history of slavery alone but also that a whole people were marked as inferior by the law. And that mark has endured. The dream of America as the great melting pot has not been realized for the Negro; because of his skin color he never even made it into the pot.

These differences in the experience of the Negro make it difficult for me to accept that Negroes cannot be afforded greater protection under the Fourteenth Amendment where it is necessary to remedy the effects of past discrimination. In the *Civil Rights Cases, supra* the Court wrote that the negro emerging from slavery must cease "to be the special favorite of the laws." 109 U.S., at 25; see p. 5. *supra.* We cannot in light of the history of the last century yield to that view. Had the Court in that case and others been willing to "do for human liberty and the fundamental rights of American citizenship, what it did . . . for the protection of slavery and the rights of the masters of fugitive salves," *id.,* at 53 (Harlan, J., dissenting), we would not need now to permit the recognition of any "special wards."

Most importantly, had the Court been willing in 1896, in *Plessey* v. *Ferguson,* to hold that the Equal Protection Clause forbids differences in treatment based on race, we would not be faced with this dilemma in 1978. We must remember, however, that the principle that the "Constitution is colorblind" appeared only in the opinion of the lone dissenter. 163 U.S., at 559. The majority of the Court rejected the principle of color blindness, and for the next 60 years, from *Plessy* to *Brown* v. *Board of Education,* ours was a Nation where, *by law,* an individual could be given "special" treatment based on the color of his skin.

It is because of a legacy of unequal treatment that we now must permit the institutions of this society to give consideration to race in making decisions about who will hold the positions of influence, affluence and prestige in America. For far too long, the doors to those positions have been shut to Negroes. If we are ever to become a fully integrated society, one in which the color of a person's skin will not determine the opportunities available to him or her, we must be willing to take steps to open those doors. I do not believe that anyone can truly look into America's past and still find that a remedy for the effects of that past is impermissible.

It has been said that this case involves only the individual, Bakke, and this University. I doubt, however, that there is a computer capable of determining the number of persons and institutions that may be affected by the decision in this case. For example, we are told by the Attorney General of the United States that at least 27 federal agencies have adopted regulations requiring recipients of federal funds to take *"affirmative action* to overcome the effects of conditions which resulted in limiting participation . . . by persons of a particular race, color, or national origin." Supplemental Brief for the United States as *Amicus Curiae* 16 (emphasis added). I cannot even guess the number of state and local governments that have set up affirmative action programs, which may be affected by today's decision.

I fear that we have come full circle. After the Civil War our government started several "affirmative action" programs. This Court in the *Civil Rights Cases* and *Plessy* v. *Ferguson* destroyed the movement toward complete equality. For almost a century no action was taken, and this nonaction was with the tacit approval of the courts. Then we had *Brown* v. *Board of Education* and the Civil Rights Acts of Congress, followed by numerous affirmative action programs. *Now,* we have this Court again stepping in, this time to stop affirmative action programs of the type used by the University of California.

Notes

Overview

1. Faustine C. Jones, *The Changing Mood in America: Eroding Commitment?* (Washington, D.C.: Howard University Press, 1977), pp. 77–78.

2. The following articles note the spread of conservatism: Robert Lekachman, "Proposition 13 and the New Conservatism," *Change* September 1978, pp. 22–27; Irving Howe, "The Right Menace," *New Republic,* 9 September 1978, pp. 12–22; Peter Connolly, "Conservative Drift in Congress," *Dissent* 26 (Winter 1979): pp. 14–17; Irving Howe, "Thunder on the Right?", *Dissent* 26 (Winter 1979): pp. 13–14. These articles praise or look favorably upon the spread of conservatism: "Why the Shift to Conservatism," *U.S. News and World Report,* 23 January 1978, pp. 24–25; "Conservative Cry—Our Time Has Come," *U.S. News and World Report,* 26 February, 1979, p. 52.

3. Lyndon B. Johnson, *The Vantage Point: Perspectives of the Presidency 1963–1969* (New York: Holt, Rinehart and Winston, 1971), p. 345; *Washington Post,* 5 January 1979, pp. A1, A10.

4. Vernon Jordan, "The New Negativism," *Newsweek;* 14 August 1978, p. 12.

5. William Watts and Lloyd A. Free, *The State of the Nation III (Lexington,Mass: Lexington Books, 1978),* p. 197.

6. See the full-page ad "Why Proposition 13 Will Work," *Los Angeles Times,* 31 May 1978, p. 28. Among the Signees were Economists Milton Friedman, Neil Jacoby, William R. Allen, Martin Anderson and Thomas Sowell.

7. See George Will, "Reverse Discrimination," *Newsweek,* 10 July 1978, p. 84; Nathan Glazer, *Affirmative Discrimination: Ethnic Inequality and Public Policy* (New York: Basic Books, 1975); Thomas Sowell, *Affirmative Action Reconsidered: Was It Necessary in Academia?* (Washington, D.C.: American Enterprise Institute for Public Policy Research, 1975); Sowell, "Bakke and the Blacklash," *Washington Star,* 8 July 1978, p. A-7.

8. "A Pointless Pressure on the Poor," *New York Times,* 27 June 1979, p. A30.

9. *New York Times,* 11 June 1979, p. B9.

10. *Los Angeles Times,* 17 October 1978, pp. 1, 18.

11. William Julius Wilson, *The Declining Significance of Race: Blacks and Changing American Institutions* (Chicago: The University of Chicago Press, 1978); Richard Barry Freeman, *Black Elite: The New Market for Highly Educated Black Americans* (New York: McGraw-Hill, 1976).

12. Louis Harris and Associates, Inc. *A Study of Attitudes Toward Racial and Religious Minorities and Toward Women* (New York: National Conference of Christians and Jews, 1978), p. 4.

13. Martin Anderson, *Welfare: The Political Economy of Welfare Reform in the United States* (Stanford, California: Hoover Institution Press), pp. 37, 39.

14. *New York Post,* 22 May 1979, p. 21.

15. Watts and Free, *The State of the Nation III,* p. 10.

16. *U.S. News and World Report,* August 1979, p. 82; *Washington Post,* 4 July 1974, p. A 25; *Los Angeles Times,* 31 July 1979, p. 6.

17. *Washington Star,* 26 July 1978, p. A-17; *Atlanta Constitution,* 18 July 1978, p. 5-A; Carl Gershman, "The World According to Andrew Young," *Commentary,* August 1978, pp. 17–24.

18. *New York Post,* 27 July 1978, p. 25; *Chicago Tribune,* 3 August 1978, Sec. 3, p. 4; Dorothy Rubinowitz, "Blacks, Jews, and New York Politics," *Commentary,* November 1978, pp. 42–48; *Chicago Tribune,* 15 August 1978, Sec. 3, p. 3; *Washington Star,* 27 March 1978, p. A-9; *Washington Star,* 5 March 1978, p. D-3; *Philadelphia Inquirer,* 21 May 1979, p. 11-A; *New York Times,* 12 April 1979, p. A23; 13 April 1979, p. 21.

19. Thomas Sowell, *Black Education: Myths and Education* (New York: David McKay Company, 1974), pp. 161–162.

20. Tom Wolfe, "The 'Me' Decade and the Third Great Awakening," *New York,* 23 August 1976, p. 40.

21. Christopher Lasch, *The Culture of Narcissism: American Life in An Age of Diminishing Expectations,* (New York: W. W. Norton and Co., 1978), pp. 4–5.

22. Ibid., p. 25.

23. Peter Marin, "The New Narcissism," *Harper's,* October 1975, pp. 47–48. Cited in Lasch, *The Culture of Narcissism,* p. 25.

24. Edwin M. Schur, *The Awareness Trap: Self-Absorption Instead of Social Change* (New York: Quadrangle Books, 1976), pp. 4–5, 182. Cited in Lasch, *The Culture of Narcissism,* pp. 25–26.

25. *New York Times,* 13 August 1979, p. A15.

26. *New York Times,* 12 November 1978, p. 22.

27. *Newsweek,* 12 September 1977, pp. 30–34.

28. Peter McGrath, "The Middle Class Is Mad as Hell," *Washingtonian,* November 1978, pp. 150–154.

29. Ibid., p. 152.

30. Ibid., p. 153

31. *Washington Star,* 20 May 1979, p. A-2.

32. *Newsweek,* 29 January 1979, p. 50.

33. *U.S. News and World Report,* 16 July 1979, p. 61.

34. *New York Times,* 23 July 1979, p. 12.

35. Douglas Miller and Marion Nowak, *The Fifties: The Way We Really Were,* (Garden City, New York: Doubleday and Company, Inc., 1977), p. 4.

36. *Washington Star,* 25 March 1979, p. E-2.

37. Ibid; Village Voice, 12 February 1979, p. 11; *Wall Street Journal,* 26 January 1979, p. 15; *Newsweek,* 2 April 1979, p. 58; *Washington Star,* 5 August 1979, p. H3; *Washington Star.*

38. Arthur M. Schlesinger, Sr. "The Tides of National Politics," cited in Eric Goldman, *Rendezvous With Destiny* (New York: Vantage Books, p. 224; Arthur M. Schlesinger, Jr. "Sources of the New Deal," in Arthur M. Schlesinger, Jr. and Morton White, eds. *Paths of American Thought* (Boston: Houghton Mifflin Company, 1963), pp. 375, 377.

39. Arthur M. Schlesinger, Jr. "Sources of the New Deal," p. 374.

40. Paul L. Murphy, "Sources and Nature of Intolerance in the 1920's, "in R. Jackson Wilson, ed., *Reform, Crisis, and Confusion, 1900–1929* (New York: Random House, 1970), p. 182.

41. Kenneth T. Jackson, "The Urban Klansman, and the Fear of Change" in Leroy Ashby and Bruce M. Stave, eds., *The Discontented Society* (Chicago: Rand McNally and Company, 1972), pp. 198–199.

42. Ibid.

43. William H. Chafe, *The American Woman: Her Changing Social, Economic, and Political Role, 1922–1970* (New York: Oxford University Press, 1972), pp. 49–50.

44. Eric Goldman, *the Crucial Decade—and After: America, 1945–1960* (New York: Vintage Books, 1960), p. 121.

45. Miller and Nowak, *The Fifties,* pp. 93–100.

46. Ibid., p. 255.

47. Richard Hofstadter, *Age of Reform* (New York: Vintage Books, 1955), pp. 12–14.

48. Hofstadter, "The Pseudo-Conservative Revolt—1955" in Daniel Bell, ed. *The Radical Right,* revised edition (Freeport, New York: Books for Libraries Press, 1971), p. 71.

49. Seymour Martin Lipset, "The Radical Right: A Problem for American Democracy" in Richard O. Curry and Thomas M. Brown, eds. *Conspiracy: The Fear of Subversion in American History* (New York: Holt, Rinehart and Winston, Inc., 1972), p. 197.

50. David Riesman and Nathan Glazer, "The Intellectuals and the Discontented Classes—1955" in Daniel Bell., ed *The Radical Right, p. 94.*

The Conservative/Neo-Conservative Impulse

1. *Washington Post.* 20 February 1979, pp. B1, B4, 31 July 1979, pp. B1, B9; *New York Post,* 13 October 1978, p. 67; *New York Times,* 21 January 1979, Sec. IV, p. 4; *Washington Star,* 9 July 1978,

p. C-3; *Washington Star,* 15 January 1979, p. A-7; Karl O'Lessker, "Neo-conservatism—Which Party's Line," *American Spectator,* March 1979, pp. 8–10; *Newsweek,* 7 November 1977, pp. 34, 36, 42; Peter Steinfels, "The Reasonable Right," *Esquire,* 13 February 1979, pp. 24–30; Geoffrey Norman, "The Godfather of Neo-conservatism (And His Family)," *Esquire,* 13 February 1979, pp. 37–42.

2. See comments in *Commentary,* September 1976, pp. 50, 61, 74; Lipset, *Commentary,* September 1978, p. 46; Norman, "The Godfather," p. 40; Steinfels, "The Reasonable Right," p. 37.

3. Amitai Etzioni, "The Neo-conservatives: Their Views of Society and Human Nature," *Current,* February 1978, pp. 20–22.

4. Jones, *The Changing Mood,* pp. 40–48; Peter Steinfels, *The Neoconservatives: The Men Who Are Changing America's Politics* (New York: Simon and Schuster, 1979), pp. 7–9; Peter Clecak, "Neo-Conservative Vision," Review of *Two Cheers for Capitalism* by Irving Kristol, *Social Policy* 9 (March/April 1979): pp. 46–52; Richard Gillam, "Intellectuals and Power," *Center Magazine* 10 (May/June 1977): pp. 15–30.

5. George H. Nash, *The Conservative Intellectual Movement in America Since 1945* (New York: Basic Books, Inc. 1976), pp. 58, 62.

6. Nash, *The Conservative Intellectual Movement,* p. 331. These ideas are found in Robert A. Nisbet, "The Dilemma of Conservatives in a Populist Society," *Policy Review* 4 (Spring 1978): 91–104; and Michael Novak's columns in the *Washington Star,* 9 July 1978, p. C-3, 8 January 1979, p. A-9, 12 January 1979, p. A-9.

7. See comments of Glazer, Kristol, Nisbet in *Commentary,* September 1976.

8. "Is America Moving Right? Ought It?: A Conversation with Irving Kristol and Arthur Schlesinger, Jr." *Public Opinion,* September/October 1978, p. 9.

9. *Wall Street Journal,* 17 July 1978, pp. 1, 17; *Chicago Tribune,* 15 November 1978, pp. 1, 4; William Simon, *A Time for Truth* (New York: Readers Digest Press, 1978), p.

10. *Newsweek,* 26 June 1978, pp. 59–60; *New York Times,* 20 May 1979, Sec. 3, pp. 4, 11.

11. Nathan Glazer, "The Limits of Social Policy," *Commentary,* September 1971, pp. 51–58; Amitai Etzioni, "Societal Overload: Sources, Components, and Corrections," *Political Science Quarterly,* 92 (Winter 1978): pp. 607–631.

12. Of the neo-conservatives, Ben Wattenberg and Nathan Glazer, although the latter to a lesser extent, are the most favorably disposed to the Great Society. However both agree that government regulatory functions should be curtailed. See *Washington Post,* 17 December 1978, pp. D1, D5.

13. See James Q. Wilson and Patricia Rachal "Can the Government Regulate Itself," *Public Interest* 46 (Winter 1977): pp. 3–14; Donald L. Horowitz, "Are the Courts Going Too Far?" *Commentary,* January 1977, pp. 37–44; Paul Weaver, "Regulation, Social Policy, and Class Conflict," *Public Interest* 50 (Winter 1978): pp. 45–63; Allan H. Meltzer and Scott F. Richard, "Why Government Grows (and Grows) in a Democracy," *Public Interest* 52 (Summer 1978): pp. 111–118; Daniel P. Moynihan, "Imperial Government," *Commentary,* June 1978, pp. 25–32; "The Sears Catalog of Litigation," *Regulation,* March/April 1979, pp. 39–48; Howard Margolis, "The Politics of Auto Emissions," *Public Interest* 49 (Fall 1977): pp. 3–21; Erigene Bardach and Lucian Pugliaresi, "The Environmental Impact Statement vs. The Real World," *Public Interest* 49 (Fall 1977): pp. 22–38; Albert L. Nichols and Richard Zeckhauser, "Government Comes to the Workplace: An Assessment of OSHA" *Public Interest* 49 (Fall 1977): pp. 39–69.

14. Nathan Glazer, *Affirmative Discrimination: Ethnic Inequality and Public Policy,* revised edition (New York: Basic Books, Inc., 1978), pp. 92–109, 208–211, 216–219; Glazer "Should Judges Administer Social Services," *Public Interest* 50 (Winter 1978): 64–80.

15. Nisbet, "The Dilemma of Conservatives," pp. 99–100; *The Washington Star,* 9 July 1978, p. C-3.

16. *Washington Star,* 12 January 1979, p. A-7, 21 April 1979; p. A-11.

17. Glazer, *Affirmative Discrimination,* pp. xii–xiii.

18. *Washington Star,* 12 January 1979, p. A-7; 21 April 1979, p. A-11; Midge Decter, "Looting and Liberal Racism," *Commentary,* September 1977, pp. 48–54.

19. Edward C. Banfield, *The Unheavenly City in the Nature and Future of Our Urban Crisis* (Boston: Little, Brown, 1970); James Q. Wilson, *Thinking About Crime* (New York: Basic Books, Inc., 1975).

The Great Society Assessed

1. William E. Simon, *A Time for Truth* (New York: Reader's Digest Press, 1978), p. 90.

2. Geoffrey Norman, "The Godfather of Neoconservatism (And His Family)," *Esquire* 13 February 1979, p. 41; *Washington Post*, 20 May 1979, p. B5.

3. Sar A. Levitan and Robert Taggart, *The Promise of Greatness* (Cambridge, Mass: Harvard University Press, 1976); Eric F. Goldman, "The Sixties, Liberally Speaking," *New Times*, 23 January 1978, pp. 6, 8, 9; Bayard Rustin, *Strategies for Freedom: The Changing Patterns of Black Protest* (New York: Columbia University Press, 1976), pp. 61–62, 67; Rochelle L. Stanfield, "Earning Their Stripes in the War on Poverty," *National Journal*, 3 March 1979, p. 348; Robert J. Samuelson, "The View from the Battlefield of the War of Poverty." *National Journal*, 3 March 1979, pp. 340–344.

4. U.S. Department of Commerce, Bureau of the Census, *The Social and Economic Status of the Black Population in the United States: An Historical View, 1790–1978* (Washington, D.C.: Government Printing Office, 1979), p. 28.

5. Martin Anderson, *Welfare: The Political Economy of Welfare Reform* (Stanford, California: Hoover Institution Press, 1978), pp. 37, 39; Martin Paglin, "Poverty in the United States: A Reevaluation," *Policy Review* 8 (Spring 1979): pp. 7–24.

6. Elliott Currie, "The New Face of Poverty," *Progressive*, January 1979, pp. 38–39.

7. Ibid., p. 39.

8. Ibid.

9. *New York Times*, 29 July 1979, Sec. IV p. 2.

10. Goldman, "The Sixties Liberally Speaking," pp. 6, 8, 9.

11. John Blum *et al*, *The National Experience: A History of the United States*, 3rd ed. (New York: Harcourt Brace Jovanovich, Inc., 1973) pp. 772, 799–800.

12. Simon, *A Time for Truth*, p. 202.

13. Cited in Levitan and Taggart, *The Promise of Greatness*, p. 124.

14. Harrell Rodgers, "Head Start—Where Are the Headlines Now?" *Dissent* 26 (Spring 1979): pp. 234–236; *New York Times*, 30 April 1978, Sec. 12, p. 9; *New York Post*, 13 August 1979, p. 19.

15. Rodgers, "Head Start," p. 235.

16. *Encore*, 5 February 1979, p. 5.

17. For example, see Paul Copperman, *The Literacy Hoax: The Decline of Reading, Writing, and Learning in the Public Schools and What We Can Do About It.* (New York: William Morrow and Company, Inc., 1978), pp. 119–123.

18. The Potomac Institute, *Central City Schooling: Money Can Make A Difference* (Washington, D.C.: The Potomac Institute, 1977), pp. 40–41.

19. Levitan and Taggart, *The Promise of Greatness*, p. 128.

20. Institute for the Study of Educational Policy, *Equal Educational Opportunity: An Assessment* (Washington, D.C.: Howard University Press, 1976), pp. 213, 217.

21. Levitan and Taggart, *The Promise of Greatness*, p. 130.

22. Lorenzo Morris, *Elusive Equality: The Status of Black Americans in Higher Education* (Washington, D.C.: Howard University Press, 1979).

23. Ibid.

24. Rodgers, "Head Start," pp. 235–236.

25. Duffy, *Domestic Affairs*, pp. 101–111. The Potomac Institute, *Central City Schooling*, p. 38.

26. Copperman, *The Literacy Hoax*, pp. 121–122.

27. The Potomac Institute, *Central City Schooling*, pp. 36–63.

28. Andrew Brimmer, "Economic Developments in the Black Community," in Eli Ginzberg and Robert M. Solow, eds. *The Great Society: Lessons for the Future* (New York: Basic Books, Inc., 1974), pp. 154–55.

29. *U.S. News and World Report*, 14 May 1979, p. 65.

30. Sar H. Levitan and Benjamin H. Johnston, *The Job Corps: A Social Experiment That Works* (Baltimore: The Johns Hopkins University Press, 1975), pp. 85, 93.

31. Ibid., pp. 101.

32. Dorothy K. Newman, Nancy J. Amidet, Barbara L. Carter, Dawn Day, William J. Kruvant, Jack S. Russell, *Protest, Politics and Prosperity: Black Americans and White Institutions, 1940–1975* (New York: Pantheon Books, 1978), p. 48.

33. Henry J. Aaron, *Politics and the Professors: The Great Society in Perspective* (Washington, D.C.: The Brookings Institution, 1978), pp. 17, 159.
34. Levitan and Taggart, *The Promise of Greatness*, pp. 274-275.

Black Progress: Myths and Realities

1. *New York Post*, 12 September 1977, p. 18; *New York Times*, 26 February 1978, p. 28; Watts and Free, *State of the Nation III*, p. 66 Harris and Associates, *Study of Attitudes*, p. 4; Gallup Opinion Index, November 1978, pp. 20-24.
2. *New York Post*, 12 September 1977, p. 18.
3. Harris and Associates, *Study of Attitudes*, pp. 2-3;
4. Ibid., p. 5.
5. Richard B. Freeman, *Black Elite: The New Market*, passim Freeman, "Black Economic Progress Since 1964" *Public Interest* 52 (Summer 1978): pp. 52-68; *New York Times*, 4 February 1979, Sec. IV, p. 19; *U.S. News and World Report*, 5 June 1978, p. 51.
6. Glazer, *Affirmative Discrimination*, pp. 127-128.
7. *Washington Post*, 13 April 1979, p. A13.
8. Institute for the Study of Educational Policy, *Equal Educational Opportunity: An Assessment*, p. 49; Institute for the Study of Educational Policy, *Equal Educational Opportunity: More Promise Than Progress* (Washington, D.C.: Howard University Press, 1978), p. 36; Michael Olivas, *The Dilemma of Access: Minorities in Two Year Colleges* (Washington, D.C.: Howard University Press, 1979.
9. Olivas, *The Dilemma of Access*, Table 2-12.
10. Morris, *Elusive Equality*.
11. *New York Times*, 25 July 1979, p. A10.
12. Ibid.
13. Compilations based upon data in the *Washington Star*, 6 July 1979, 6 July 1979, pp. A1, A5.
14. *Chicago Tribune*, 19 October 1978, pp. 1, 10.
15. Peter Drucker, "Unemployment Is Not As High As You Think," *Washington Post*, 12 November 1978, p. B3; James S. Henry, "Lazy, Young, Female and Black: The New Conservative Theories of Unemployment," *Working Papers for a New Society*, May/June 1978, pp. 55-65; James S. Henry, "Hallelujah I'm a Bum: The New Conservative Theories of Unemployment," *Working Papers for a New Society*, May 1979, pp. 71-79.
16. Henry, "Hallelujah," p. 74; *New York Times*, 23 July 1979, p. 12.
17. Thomas, Sowell, "Racism, Quotas and the Front Door," *Wall Street Journal*, 28 July 1979, p. 8; Walter Williams, "Government Sanctioned Restraints That Reduce Economic Opportunities for Minorities," *Policy Review* 1 (Fall 1977): pp. 28-37; Finis Welch, "The Rising Impact of Minimum Wages," *Regulation* November/December 1978.
18. *Los Angeles Times*, 24 December 1978, p. 8.
19. *Washington Star*, 24 June 1979, pp. C1, C3.
20. Bureau of the Census, *The Social and Economic Status of the Black Population*, p. 186.
21. Sowell, "Are Quotas Good for Blacks," *Commentary*, June 1978, p. 40; Sowell, "Myths About Minorities," *Commentary*, August 1979, p. 37.
22. National Center for Education Statistics, *The Condition of Education—1979* (Washington, D.C.: Government Printing Office, 1979), p. 216.
23. Ibid.
24. *Atlanta Constitution*, 14 December 1978, p. 2-B.
25. *New York Amsterdam News*, 19 May 1979, p. 53.
26. Robert Hill, "Economic Status of Black Families" in National Urban League, *The State of Black American* 1979 (New York: National Urban League, 1979), p. 31.
27. Ibid., pp. 31-32.
28. *New York Times*, 17 May 1979, p. B11.
29. Wilson, *The Declining Significance of Race*, pp. 129-134.
30. *Boston Globe*, 20 August 1979, p. 25.
31. *New York Times*, 22 March 1978, p. 33.

32. Charles V. Willie, "The Inclining Significance of Race," *Society* (July/Augst 1978): pp. 10, 12; *Boston Globe,* 20 August 1979, pp. 23, 25.

33. Cited in Joel Dreyfuss, "Black Progress: Myth and Ghetto Reality," *Progressive,* November 1977, p. 23.

34. Edward J. Burke, "3,700 Partners, 12 Are Black," *National Law Journal,* 2 July 1979, pp. 1, 15.

35. Ibid., p. 15.

36. Nick Kotz, "The Minority Struggle for a Place in the Newsroom," *Columbia Journalism Review* 17 (March/April 1979): pp. 23-24.

37. Wilson, *The Declining Significance of Race,* p. 154.

38. Glazer, liner notes, on jacket of *The Declining Significance of Race.*

39. Sowell, review of *The Declining Significance of Race* by William J. Wilson, *Policy Review* 7 (Winter 1979): 120.

40. Williams, "Race and Economics," *Public Interest* 53 (Fall 1978): 149-150.

41. See Stephen Birmingham, *Certain People: America's Black Elite* (Boston: Little, Brown, and Co., 1977); William Brashler, "The Black Middle Class: Making It," *New York Times Magazine,* 3 December, 1978.

42. Harriette Pipes McAdoo, "Black Kinship," *Psychology Today* 12 (May 1979): 67, 69, 70, 79, 110.

43. Earl Caldwell, "The Rising Status of Commitment," *Black Enterprise,* December 1978, p. 42.

44. Ibid.

45. Alan D. Monroe, *Public Opinion in America* (New York: Dodd, Mead and Co., 1975), pp. 92-93.

46. Ibid.

Attacks on American Public Education

1. "Speculating in the Open Market," *New York Times,* 20 August 1979, p. A20.

2. See John E. Fleming, *The Lengthening Shadow of Slavery: A Historical Justification for Affirmative Action for Blacks in Higher Education* (Washington, D.C.: Howard University Press, 1976) passim; David Nasaw, *Schooled to Order: A Social History of Public Schooling in the United States* (New York: Oxford University Press, 1979), *passim.*

3. George Gallup, "The 10th Annual Gallup Poll on the Public's Attitudes Toward the Public Schools," *Phi Delta Kappan* 60 (September 1978): p. 35.

4. Ibid.

5. Christopher Jencks *et al., Inequality: A Reassessment of the Effect of Family and Schooling in America* (New York: Basic Books, Inc., 1972), pp. 8-9.

6. Samuel Bowles and Herbert Gintis, *Schooling in Capitalist America: Educational Reform and the Contradictions of Economic Life* (New York: Basic Books, Inc., 1975), p. 14.

7. John U. Ogbu, Minority Education and Caste: *The American System in Cross-Cultural Perspective* (New York: Academic Press, 1978), pp. 213-315, 350.

8. *Washington Post,* 22 August 1979, p. A2.

9. Ogbu, *Minority Education and Caste,* p. 100; *New York Times,* 24 August 1979, p. A14.

10. Lasch, *The Culture of Narcissism,* pp. 125, 127.

11. Copperman, *The Literacy Hoax,* pp. 15-16.

12. Nancy Hicks, "Public Education: What's Happening to the Children," *Black Enterprise,* September 1978, pp. 29-33; *Washington Star,* 11 July 1979, pp. B1, B3; *Chicago Tribune,* 26 July 1979, p. 3.

13. Gene I. Maeroff, "The Cupboard Is Still Bare in Toledo," *Phi Delta Kappan* 59 (February 1978): 380.

14. William R. Grant, "Detroit School Finance: A Perils of Pauline Melodrama, *Phi Delta Kappan* 59 (February 1978): p. 384.

15. Maeroff, "The Cupboard Is Still Bare," p. 381; *Newsweek,* 25 September 1978, p. 105; *New York Times,* 12 November 1978, p. 24.

16. David Sears, Carl Hensler, and Leslie K. Speer "Whites' Opposition to Busing: Self-Interest or Symbolic Politics?" *American Political Science Review* 73 (June 1979): pp. 382-383.

17. National Center for Education Statistics, *The Condition of Education 1979* (Washington, D.C.: Government Printing Office, 1979), p. 142.

18. *Newsweek,* 23 October 1978, p. 108; *Atlanta Journal and Constitution,* 29 April 1979, p. 4-B.

The Opposition to Busing

1. See *New York Times,* 23 May 1979, p. A23; Lino Graglia, "The Supreme Court's Abuse of Power," *National Review,* 21 July 1978, pp. 892–896; Nathan Glazer, *Affirmative Discrimination,* p. 98.

2. Graglia, "The Supreme Court's Abuse," pp. 892–896; Glazer, *Affirmative Discrimination,*; pp. 105, 106, 107; Sowell, "Are Quotas Good for Blacks, *Commentary* June 1978, p. 42.

3. Sowell, "Are Quotas Good for Blacks," p. 42.

4. See *Journal of Negro Education* 47 (Winter 1978). The theme of the issue "Desegregation in the 1970s: A Candid Discussion."

5. Derrick Bell, "The Curse of *Brown* on Black," *First World* 2 (Spring 1978): 14–18; Bell, "The Community Role in Educating Poor Black Children," *Education Digest* 44 (December 1978): 58–61.

6. Bell, "The Curse of *Brown,*" pp. 16–17; Bell, "The Community Role," pp. 59–60.

7. See Barbara A. Sizemore, "Educational Research and Desegregation: Significance for the Black Community," *Journal of Negro Education* 47 (Winter 1978): pp. 58–68.

8. *New York Times,* 11 June 1978, p. 27; Diane Ravitch, "The White Flight' Controversy," *Public Interest* 51 (Spring 1978): pp. 135–149; *Washington Post,* 8 December 1978, p. A19; *Chicago Tribune,* 17 September 1978, Sec. 2, pp. 1, 5. David J. Armor, *White Flight, Demographic Transition and the Future of School Desegregation* (Santa Monica, California: Rand Corporation, 1978).

9. Christine Rossell, "White Flight: Pros and Cons," *Social Policy* 9 (November/December 1978): pp. 46–51.

10. Ernest Erber, "White Flight and Political Retreat," *Dissent* 26 (Winter 1979): pp. 53–57.

11. Ibid.

12. Ravitch, "The 'White Flight' Controversy," p. 140.

13. *Washington Post,* 8 December 1978, p. A19; *Chicago Tribune,* 17 September 1978, Sec. 2, pp. 1, 5.

14. Armor, *White Flight,* p.

15. *Los Angeles Times,* 25 December 1978, Part II, pp. 1, 5.

16. *Los Angeles Times,* 28 July 1979, Part II, p. 12.

17. *Los Angeles Times,* 10 June 1979, pp. 1, 16.

18. *Los Angeles Times,* 10 December 1978, p. 20.

19. U.S. Commission on Civil Rights, *Desegregation of the Nation's Public Schools: A Status Report,* p. 9.

20. *New York Times,* 25 July 1978, pp. A1, A14.

21. *New York Times,* 16 March 1978, p. 34; *U.S. News and World Report,* 8 May 1978, p. 47.

22. *Atlanta Constitution,* 30 March 1979, pp. 14-A, 15-A; *Los Angeles Times,* 14 May 1979, pp. 15, 19.

23. *Los Angeles Times,* 11 March 1979, Part VI, p. 3.

24. *Boston Globe,* 25 June 1979, p. 6.

25. Charles B. McMillian, "Magnet Education in Boston," *Phi Delta Kappan,* 59 (November 1977): Daniel U. Levine and Nolan Estes, "Magnet Education in Dallas," *Phi Delta Kappan,* 59 (November 1977):

26. Robert L. Crain and Rita E. Mahard, *Desegregation and Black Achievement* (Santa Monica, California: The Rand Corporation, 1977), p. 8.

27. Ibid., p. 27.

28. Ibid., p. 32–33.

29. *Washington Post,* 9 September 1973, p. A12; George H. Gallup, *The Gallup Poll: Public Opinion 1972-1977,* Vol. 1, *1972–75* (Wilmington, Del.: Scholarly Resources Inc., 1978), p. 566.

30. Watts and Free, *The State of the Nation III,* p. 190.

31. Everett C. Ladd, Jr. "Profile of Social Attitudes in the 70's," *Public Opinion* 1 (July/August 1978): 26.

32. *Atlanta Constitution,* (Special News Report), 16 May 1979, p. 9.
33. Louis Harris and Associates, *A Study of Attitudes,* pp. 38–39.
34. Ibid., p. 40.
35. *New York Times,* 8 July 1979, Sec. IV, p. 1.

Tuition Tax Credits and Education Vouchers

1. *U.S. News and World Report,* 30 April 1979, p. 48.
2. *Washington Post,* 3 May 1978, p. A5.
3. Ibid.
4. *New York Times,* 14 June 1978, Sec. IV, p. 9.
5. Ibid.
6. Speech by Rep. William Ford, 1 June 1978. Cited in *Congressional Digest* 58 (January 1979): p. 27.
7. *Washington Post,* 2 July 1978, p. B-5; *Atlanta Constitution,* 25 August 1978, p. 5-A.
8. Morris, *Elusive Equality.*
9. Argument by Senator Ernest F. Hollings, 14 August 1978. Cited in *Congressional Digest* 58 (January 1979): p. 25.
10. Statement of Senator Daniel P. Moynihan before House Ways and Means Committee, 21 February 1978. Cited in *Congressional Digest* 58 (January 1979): pp. 22, 24.
11. Sowell, "Tuition Tax Credits: A Social Revolution," *Policy Review* 4 (Spring 1978): 79–83; Williams, "Tuition Tax Credits: Other Benefits" *Policy Review* 4 (Spring 1978): pp. 85–89; *Washington Post,* 20 June 1978, p. A3.
12. Robert W. Cottrol, "Catholic Schools: Vanishing Hope for Quality Education," *Sepia,* July 1979, p. 80.
13. Sowell, "Tuition Tax Credits," pp. 80–82; Williams, "Tuition Tax Credits," pp. 86–88; *Washington Post,* 20 June 1978, p. A3.
14. *Pittsburgh Courier,* 8 July 1978, p. 8.
15. *Pittsburgh Courier,* 29 April 1978, p. 5.
16. *Pittsburgh Courier,* 3 June 1978, p. 8.
17. *Washington Post,* 8 August 1978, p. A2.
18. Ibid.
19. *New York Times,* 30 May 1979, p. B1.
20. *Washington Star,* 30 May 1979, p. A10.
21. Milton Friedman, *Capitalism and Freedom* (Chicago: The University of Chicago Press, 1962), pp. 89, 91; Sowell, *Black Education,* pp. 242–250; Christopher Jencks, "Giving Parents Money for Schooling: Education Vouchers," *Phi Delta Kappan* 51 (September 1970):
22. Ibid.
23. Daniel Weiler, *A Public School Voucher Demonstration: The First Year at Alum Rock* (Santa Monica, California: Rand Corporation 1974), pp. 171, 181.
24. Ibid., p. 183.
25. Ibid., p. 175.
26. David K. Cohen and Eleanor Farrar, "Power to the Parents?—The Story of Education Vouchers," *Public Interest* 48 (Summer 1977): 89–90.
27. Patricia M. Lines, "The Tuition Voucher: A Means to Secure Both Desegregation and Parental Choice," *Ripon Forum* 15 (June 1979): 11, 12.
28. Ibid.
29. John E. Coons and Stephen D. Sugarman, *Education by Choice: The Case for Family Control* (Berkeley, California: University of California Press, 1978).
30. Ibid., pp. 109, 112.
31. *New York Times,* 28 July 1979, p. A6.

Competency Based Testing

1. *New York Times,* 12 October 1977, p. 14.
2. Joseph and Helen Featherstone, "The Cult of Measurement," *Working Papers for a New*

Society, March/April 1978, pp. 10, 11, 88; *Los Angeles Times,* 17 December 1978, Part X, p. 10; *Washington Post,* 5 July 1979, p. D 10.

3. Sylvia T. Johnson, *The Measurement Mystique: Issues in Selection for Professional Schools and Employment* (Washington, D.C.: ISEP, 1979), p. 3.

4. James J. Gallagher, "Minimum Competency: The Setting of Educational Standards," *Educational Evaluation and Policy Analysis.* 1 (Number One 1979): p. 64.

5. Walt Haney and George Madaus, "Making Sense of the Competency Testing Movement" *Harvard Educational Review* 48 (November 1978): p. 464.

6. Ibid., pp. 465, 468.

7. *New York Times,* 24 July 1978, pp. A1, A11; 25 February 1979, Sec. IV, p. 18; 19 March 1979, pp. A1, D11; 22 April 1979, Sec. 12, p. 19.

8. *Washington Star,* 11 July 1979, pp. B-1, B-3; *Chicago Tribune,* 26 July 1979, p. 3.

9. Merle Steven McCluny, "Are Competency Testing Programs Fair? Legal? *Phi Delta Kappan* 59 (February 1978): p. 398.

10. Washington Star, 28 April 1978, p. A-9; Pamela George, "The Competency Controversy," *Southern Exposure* 7 (Summer 1979): p. 16.

11. *New York Times,* 11 Janurary 1979, p. A16.

12. *Time,* 30 July 1979, p. 66; *New York Times,* 14 July 1979, p. 5; *Los Angeles Times,* 14 July 1979, p. 11.

13. *Washington Star,* 28 April 1978, p. A-9; *Pittsburgh Courier,* 12 August 1978, p. 8; *Atlanta Constitution,* 19 March 1979, p. 5-A; *Newsweek,* 28 May 1979, p. 98.

Proposition 13 and the Tax Revolt

1. Quoted in Mervin Field, "Sending a Message: Californians Strike Back" *Public Opinion* 1 (July/August 1978): p. 3.

2. Robert J. Samuelson, "The New Ideology," *National Journal,* 21 October 1978, p. 1686.

3. *Washington Star,* 21 February 1979, p. G-1.

4. Mason Gaffney, "An Alternative Reform," *Center Magazine* 11 (November/December 1978): 21, 22.

5. Joan C. Baratz and Joy H. Moskowitz, "Proposition 13: How and Why It Happened," *Phi Delta Kappan* 60 (September 1978): p. 9.

6. Seymour Martin Lipset and Earl Raub, "The Message of Proposition 13" *Commentary,* September 1978, pp. 42–46; Milton Friedman, "The Limitations of Tax Limitation," *Policy Review* 5 (Summer 1978): 8; Daniel Orr "Proposition 13: Tax Reform's Lexington Bridge?" *Policy Review* 6 (Fall 1978): pp. 58–59.

7. *Los Angeles Times,* 19 June 1978, p. 13.

8. Field, "Sending a Message," p. 6; *Los Angeles Times,* 1 September 1978, p. 26.

9. Joel Dreyfuss, "Is Proposition 13 Doomsday for Blacks," *Black Enterprise,* January 1979, p. 50; *Boston Globe,* 20 August 1979, p. 25.

10. "Me First," *New Republic,* 17 June 1978, p. 5.

11. *Pittsburgh Courier,* 2 September 1978, p. 8.

12. *Washington Post,* 11 June 1978, p. C7.

13. *Los Angeles Times,* 19 June 1978, p. 13.

14. *Los Angeles Times,* 3 June 1979, p. 24.

15. *Chicago Tribune,* 10 June 1979, Sec. 2, pp. 1, 2.

16. *New York Times,* 7 November 1978, p. 22.

17. Picture reprinted in *New York Times,* 4 June 1979, p. B15.

18. Freeman, *The Black Elite,* pp. 151.

19. *Black Enterprise,* September 1978, p. 63.

20. Ibid.

21. *New York Amsterdam News,* 19 May 1979, p. 53.

22. *Los Angeles Times,* 3 June 1979, p. 24.

23. *Los Angeles Times,* 19 May 1979, Part II, p. 12.

24. *Los Angeles Times,* 3 March 1979, p. 22.

25. *Los Angeles Times,* 30 November 1978, p. 3.
26. *Chronicle of Higher Education,* 19 March 1979, p. 2.
27. *Chronicle of Higher Education,* 29 May 1979, pp. 3, 4.
28. Lavin, David; Alba, Richard; and Silberstein, Richard. "Ethnicity and Equality: The Fate of Ethnic Groups Under an Open Access Model of Higher Education." *Harvard Educational Review* (1979).
29. John E. Fleming, Gerald R. Gill, David Swinton, *The Case for Affirmative Action for Blacks in Higher Education* (Washington, D.C.: Howard University Press, 1978), p. 198.
30. *Chronicle of Higher Education,* 29 May 1979, p. 4.

Affirmative Action: *Bakke* and *Weber* Cases

1. For background on the *Bakke* case, see Institute for the Study of Educational Policy, *The Bakke Case Primer,* 1977; Joel Dreyfuss and Charles H. Lawrence III, *The Bakke Case: The Politics of Inequality* (New York: Harcourt Brace Jovanovich, Inc., 1979).
2. For background on the *Weber* case, see Affirmative Action Coordinating Center, *Affirmative Action,* 1979; Steven V. Roberts, "The *Bakke* Case Moves to the Factory," *New York Times Magazine,* 25 February 1979, pp. 36–38, 84, 86, 100, 101.
3. *New York Amsterdam News,* 1 July 1978, p. 1.
4. *Pittsburgh Courier,* 8 July 1978, pp. 1, 5.
5. *Washington Star,* 29 June 1978, pp. A1, A8.
6. *Time,* 10 July 1978, p. 15; *Atlanta Constitution,* 10 July 1978, p. 5-A.
7. *Newsweek,* 10 July 1978, p. 20.
8. *Boston Globe,* 29 June 1978, p. 28.
9. *Pittsburgh Courier,* 15 July 1978, p. 8.
10. *Pittsburgh Courier,* 5 August 1978, p. 8.
11. *Washington Afro American,* 4 July 1978, p. 2.
12. *Washington Post,* 3 July 1978, p. A-23.
13. *Washington Star,* 29 June 1978, pp. A1, A8.
14. *Time,* 10 July 1978, p. 16.
15. *Washington Star,* 8 July 1978, p. A-7.
16. *Washington Star,* 29 June 1978, p. A-8.
17. Robert H. Bork, "A Murky Future," *Regulation,* September/October 1978, pp. 36–39; Philip B. Kurland, "Bakke's Wake," *Chicago Bar Record* 60 (September/October 1978): 82.
18. George F. Will, "Reverse Discrimination," *Newsweek,* 10 July 1979, p. 84.
19. Allan P. Sindler, "The Court's Three Decisions," *Regulation* September/October 1978, p. 18.
20. Michael Novak, "Questions for the Court," *Regulation,* September/October 1978, p. 34.
21. "Justice Marshall's Dissent in *Bakke,*" *Freedomways* 18 (Third Quarter 1978): pp. 127–136; Dreyfuss and Lawrence, *The Bakke Case,* pp. 222-225.
22. See *Harvard Civil Rights—Civil Liberties Review* 14 (Spring 1979); entire issue is devoted to *Bakke.*
23. *New York Times,* 14 February 1979, p. A23.
24. Cited in *AACC News: Newsletter of the Affirmative Action Coordinating Center,* November 1978, p. 7.
25. Ibid.
26. *New York Times,* 10 November 1978, p. B2, 17 December 1978, p. 52, 14 February 1979, p. A23; *Washington Post,* 7 December 1978, pp. A1, A8; *Los Angeles Times,* 22 October 1978, Part II, p. 1; 11 March 1979, pp. 3, 22; *Chicago Tribune,* 20 October 1978, p. 3.
27. *Washington Post,* 7 December 1978, pp. A1, A8.
28. *Pittsburgh Courier,* 9 December 1978, p. 5.
29. *Washington Post,* 9 January 1979, p. A8.
30. *Washington Post,* 8 October, 1978, p. A13.
31. *Washington Post,* 7 December 1978, pp. A1, A8.
32. *Washington Post,* 7 December 1978, p. A8; *New York Times,* 10 November 1978, p. B2, 14 February 1979, p. A23.

33. *Chronicle of Higher Education,* 30 July 1979, p. 1.

34. *New York Times,* 3 December 1978, p. 45.

35. Ibid., *Washington Post,* 8 October 1978, p. A13.

36. *Chronicle of Higher Education,* 1 July 1979, p. 13.

37. Ibid.

38. Anti-Defamation League of B'nai B'rith, *A Study of Post-Bakke, Admissions Policies in Medical, Dental and Law Schools Throughout the United States.* (New York: Anti-Defamation League of B'nai B'rith, 1979), pp. 1, 2.

39. Ibid., p. 3.

40. Ibid., p. 4.

41. *New York Times,* 10 November 1978, p. B2, 14 February 1979, p. A23; *Los Angeles Times,* 11 March 1979, p. 22.

42. Derrick Bell, *"Bakke* and the Black Colleges: Compounding the Racial Ironies," unpublished paper, 1978.

43. *Atlanta Journal and Constitution,* 22 April 1979, p. 12-A.

44. Anti-Defamation League, *A Study of Post-Bakke Admissions Policies,* p. 10.

45. Ibid.

46. *United Steelworkers of America, AFL-CIO-CLC* v. *Weber*

47. *Washington Post,* 1 July 1979, p. C7; *Washington Star,* 3 July 1979, p. A-11; *Chicago Tribune,* 5 July 1979, Sec. 3, p. 5; *New York Post,* 5 July 1979, p. 27; Carl Cohen, "Justice Debased: The Weber Decision" *Commentary,* September 1979, pp. 43–53.

48. *New York Times,* 17 August 1979, p. A13.

49. *Washington Post,* 2 July 1979, p. A23; *Washington Star,* 4 July 1979, p. A-7.

50. *Atlanta Constitution,* 28 June 1979, p. 15-A.

51. *Washington Post,* 14 June 1979, p. A-3.

52. The bill alluded to is S. 1469 introduced into the Senate on 9 July 1979 by Senator Orrin Hatch, Republic of Utah.

Index

Aaron, Henry J., 23
Advancing Equality of Opportunity:
A Matter of Justice (Smith, ed.),
x
Affirmative Action, 2, 4, 63–70,
passim; attacks on, 12; in
employment, 70; programs, xiii, 3,
passim
Aid to Families with Dependent
Children, 4, 20
Alum Rock (Calif.), education voucher
experiment in, 51–52
Amendments, Constitutional:
Fifteenth, 76, 77; Fourteenth,
76, 77, 80, 81, 82; Thirteenth, 76
Amendments, legislative. *See names of*
specific amendments
American Enterprise Institute for
Public Policy Research, 16
American Jewish Committee, 65
American Jewish Congress, 65
American Telephone and Telegraph
Company, 69
Anderson, Martin, 6, 19
Armor, David, 42, 43, 45
Associated General Contractors of
California v. *Secretary of*
Commerce, 66
Atlanta (Georgia) Board of Education,
50
Atlanta Constitution, poll on busing,
45
Attitudes toward social change: of
academicians and journalists, 4;
of the affluent, 7; of the American
populace, 3, 4; of the American

polulace in the 1950s, 11–12; of
blacks, 35; of Congress, 4–5; and
the disadvantaged, 72; of the
"Woodstock generation"
The Awareness Trap: Self-Absorption
Instead of Social Change (Schur),
7

Banfield, Edward, 14, 17, 18, 19
Basic Educational Opportunity
Grants, 22, 49
Becker, Henry, 50
Bell, Daniel, 14
Bell, Derrick, 42, 68
Bell, Griffin, 82
Berkowitz, Bernard, 7
Berry, Mary, 56
Black codes, 77
Black Elite: The New Market for
Highly Educated Black
Americans (Freeman), 5, 29–30
"Black Experiences vs. Black
Expectations," EEOC report,
31–32
Blacks: black perception of progress
of, 25–26; economic status of, 79;
in the professions, 31–34, 79 (*see*
also names of individual
professions); progress of, 25–35,
27 (figure); white perception of
progress of, 25, 26; as voters, 35
B'nai B'rith, Anti-Defamation League
of, 67, 68
Board of Education v. *Swann,* 81

Bork, Robert H., 65
Born-again populism, xi
Boston (Mass.), busing in, 41, 44, 45
Bowles, Samuel, 37
Brennan, William Joseph, Jr., 65, 69
Brimmer, Andrew, 22, 60
Brown v. *Board of Education of Topeka*, 25, 41-42, 46, 79, 82, 83
Buchanan, Patrick, 69
Buckley, William, 69
Bureau of Refugees, Freedmen, and Abandoned Lands, 77, 80
Burke, Edmund, 15
Busing, xii, 2, 3, 4, 41-46; as abuse of judicial power, 42; black opposition to, 42; black support of, 45; Congressional opposition to, 41, 44; and educational achievement, 71; and educational opportunity, 40, 44-45; neo-conservative attitude toward, 16; opposition to, 12, 39; and race, 38-39; voluntary, 43-44; and white flight, 42-43, 44
Byrd Amendment, 4, 44
Byrne v. *Public Funds for Public Schools*, 51

Califano v. *Webster*, 81
Califano v. *Goldfarb*, 81
California, University of, 81, 82, 83; law school at Los Angeles, 66, 68; medical school at Davis, 66
Carter, James Earl, xi, 3, 6, 22, 34
The Case for Affirmative Action for Blacks in Higher Education (Fleming *et al.*), 61
The Changing Mood in America: Eroding Commitment? (Jones), x
Chanler, John W., 80
Charlestown News and Courier, 78
Charlotte (N.C.), busing in, 45
Chicago (Ill.), white flight from, 43

Cincinnati (Ohio), school tax levies and race in, 39
Civil Rights Act of 1875, 77
Civil Rights Act of 1964, xi, 20; and college attendance of blacks, 21; Title VII of the, 69, 70
Civil Rights Acts (reconstruction era), 77, 83
Civil Rights Cases, 77, 82, 83
Civil Rights Movement: gains derived from, 19; and the progress of Blacks, 25, 31
Civil War, 77, 83
Civil War Amendments, 77
Clark, Kenneth, 31
Cleveland (Ohio), school tax levies and race in, 39
Cohen, Carl, 69
Cohen, David K., 52
Coleman, James, 42, 45
College: attendance of Blacks, 25; costs and family income, 47, 48 (table); parental attitudes toward costs of, 47-48
College Entrance Examination Board, 47
College Work Study Program, 22
Columbia Journalism Review, 34
Columbus (Ohio): busing in, 46; school tax levies and race in, 39
Columbus Board of Education v. *Penick*, 46
Communism, fear of, 10
Competency based testing, xiii, 12, 54-56; and Black students, 55-56; defined, 54; and educational opportunity, 40, 55-56; and dropout rate, 55-56; in Florida, 55-56; shortcomings of, 38
Comprehensive Employment and Training Act, 23
Congress, acts of. *See names of individual acts*
Congressional Black Caucus, 34

Congressional Budget Office, 47, 48
Congressional Globe, 80
Conservatism, x; defined, 1-2, 2-3;
    and neo-conservatism, 14-17 (*see
    also* Neo-conservatism); in the
    1920s, 10; in the 1950s, 10
Constitution of the U.S., 49, 75, 76;
    equal protection clause of the, 82
Conyers, John, 34
Coons, John E., 52
Copperman, Paul, 22
Council on Legal Educational
    Opportunity, 66-67
Crain, Robert, 45
*The Culture of Narcissism: American
    Life in an Age of Diminishing
    Expectations* (Lasch), 38

Dallas (Tex.), magnet schools in, 44
Dayton (Ohio), busing in, 46; school
    tax levies and race in, 39
Dayton Board of Education v.
    Brinkman, 46
Death at an Early Age (Kozol), 44
Declaration of Independence, 76
The Declining Significance of Race
    (Wilson), 5, 31, 32
Decter, Midge, 14
DeFunis, Marco, 65
DeFunis v. *Odegaard,* 63
Dellums, Ronald, 64
DeLone, Richard, 37
Democracy in America (Tocqueville),
    15
Demonstrations, 72
Desegregation and Black educational
    achievement, 45
Detroit Edison, 69
Detroit (Mich.), school tax levies and
    race in, 39
Detroit Police Officers Association v.
    Young, 64
Dewey, John, 11
Dred Scott v. *Sandford,* 76

Eagleton-Biden Amendment, 4, 44
Economic Opportunity Act of 1964, xi
*Education by Choice: The Case for
    Family Control* (Coons and
    Sugarman), 52
Education vouchers, xii, xiii, 12, 42,
    43, 51-53; in California, 51-52;
    and Congress, 53; defined, 51;
    and educational opportunity, 40,
    52, 53; and the IRS, 53; and
    Proposition 13, 52; and race,
    38-39; and white flight, 53
*VIII Messages and Papers of the
    Presidents,* 80
Eisenhower, Dwight David, xi
Elementary and Secondary Education
    Act of 1965, xi; funding for Title
    I of, 22; success of Title I of, 21
Emancipation, 76-77
Employment of Black college
    graduates, 29-30
Equal Employment Opportunity
    Commission, report (1977), 31-32
Equal opportunity, 2, *passim*; in
    education denied, 78
Equal Rights Amendment, 3
Esch Amendment, 4, 44

Fair Deal, xi, 3, 10
Fair Housing Act of 1968, xi, 20
Farrar, Eleanor, 52
Feldstein, Martin, 28-29
Feminism, reaction to in the 1920s, 10
Field Foundation, 19
Fleming, John E., 61
Food Stamp program, 4, 19
Ford, Gerald R., xi
Ford Foundation, xi, xiv
Franklin, John Hope, 75, 76
Free, Lloyd H., 6, 45
Freeman, Richard Barry, 5, 29-30
Friedman, Milton, 15, 51
From Slavery to Freedom (Franklin),
    75
Fullilove v. *Kreps,* 63, 66

Gallop Poll on public confidence in public schools, 36
Garrity, W. Arthur, 44
Gill, Gerald R., x, xi, xii, xiii
Gintis, Herbert, 37
Glazer, Nathan, 12, 14, 16, 17, 26, 29, 32, 42, 65
Goldman, Eric F., 10, 11, 58
Goode, Victor, 67
Graglia, Lino A., 42
Great Depression, xi, 9
Great Society, xi, xii, 3, 37, 71, 72, *passim*; assessment of programs, 18–24; attacks on programs, 2, 6; benefits of programs, 2; conservative/neo-conservative attitude toward programs, 15, 17; funding of programs, 19–20; programs, 23–24, 62 (*see also names of individual programs*); programs viewed as failures, 18; programs viewed as successes, 19, 20
Green v. *County School Board*, 81

Hamilton, Charles, 35
Hammond (Ind.), busing in, 44
Harlan, John Marshall, 77, 78, 82
Harris, Louis and Associates, 45–46; 1977 poll, 25; 1978 poll, 5–6, 25–26
Harvard Civil Rights–Civil Liberties Law Review, 65
Hayakawa, S. I., 6
Head Start program, xii, 2, 37, 71, 72; benefits of, 20–21; funding of, 22
Henderson, Wade J., 66
Hendricks, Thomas A., 80
Higher Education Act of 1965, xi; amendments to, 1972, 21–22; and college attendance of Blacks, 21; and financial assistance, 22; Title III of, 21–22
Hofstadter, Richard, 11–12
Holman, M. Carl, 64

Hooks, Benjamin, 8, 64, 66, 69, 70
Howard University, ix, xiv; Institute for the Study of Educational Policy, ix, x, xiv, 64; National Advisory Board of the ISEP, ix, x, xiii, xiv; program objectives of the ISEP, ix; School of Dentistry, 68
How to Be Your Own Best Friend (Newman and Berkowitz), 7
How to Say No Without Feeling Guilty, 7
Human rights, denial of, 75–76
Humphrey–Hawkins bill, 31; Black support for, 34
Huntington, Samuel P., 14
Hyde Amendment, 4

Illinois, University of, law school, 66
Income, of Blacks and whites compared, 29, 30–31, 30 (figure)
Inequality, (Jencks *et al.*), 37
Inflation, effects of, 8–9

Jackson, Jesse, 64
Jarvis, Howard, 59
Jarvis–Gann initiative. *See* Proposition 13
Jefferson, Thomas, 76
Jencks, Christopher, 37, 51, 52
Jim Crow: Bible, 78; laws, 78, 79; laws and the federal government, 78
Job Corps, 2; successes of, 22–23
Johns Hopkins University, 50
Johnson, Andrew, 80
Johnson, Lyndon B., xi, 3, 22, 24
Jones, Faustine, x, 2
Jordan, Vernon, 3–4, 31, 50, 56, 59, 64, 66, 69–70
Journalists, Black and minority, 32, 33–34 (table)

Kennedy, John F., xi
Keynesian economics, 15

Kilpatrick, James J., 69
Kluger, R., 75, 78
Kozol, Jonathan, 44
Kristol, Irving, 14, 15, 18, 19
Ku Klux Klan, 10
Kurland, Philip B., 65

Lamar (S.C.), busing in, 41
Lasch, Christopher, 7, 38
Lawyers, Black, 32
Levitan, Sar A., 21, 24
Lipset, Seymour Martin, 12, 14
Looking Out for Number One (Ringer), 7
Los Angeles (Calif.): busing in, 41; Permits With Transportation program in, 43; Proposition 13 and education in, 60-61; voluntary busing in, 43
Los Angeles Times/CBS, 59
Louisville (Ky.), busing in, 41, 44, 45
Lowery, Joseph E., 69

McAdoo, Harriette, 35
McCarthyism, 11, 12
McDaniel v. *Barresi*, 81
McDougall, James A., 80
McLaurin v. *Oklahoma State Regents*, 79
Mahard, Rita, 45
Manpower Development and Training Act, 22
Marches, 72
Marshall, Thurgood, 65; text of dissenting opinion in *Regents of the University of California* v. *Allan Bakke*, 75-83
Martin, Peter, 7
Mays, Benjamin, 50
Medicaid, 4
Medical schools, Black enrollment in, 67
Medicare, 15
Merritt College, Black faculty of, 61

Middle class: benefits derived from government spending, 58; income of and inflation, 8
Middle Income Student Aid Act, 49
Minority Education and Caste (Ogbu), 37
"The Minority Struggle for a Place in the Newsroom," *Columbia Journalism Review*, 34
Missouri Compromise, 76
Monroe, Alan, 35
Morgan v. *Virginia*, 79
Moynihan, Daniel P., 14, 48, 51

Nashville (Tenn.), Head Start program, 20
National Advisory Council on Economic Opportunity, 9
National Association for the Advancement of Colored People, 8, 44
National Conference of Black Lawyers, 66, 67
National Law Journal, 31
National Office for Black Catholics, 50
National Opinion Research Center, 45
National Urban Coalition, 64
National Urban League, 3-4, 28
Neo-Conservatism, 14-17; and the concept of a conservative welfare state, 15; defined, 14-15; racial attitude of, 17
Neo-conservative deal, xi
New Deal, xi, 3, 10-11, 15
New Frontier, xi, 3
"The New Ideology" (Samuelson), *National Journal*, 58
Newman, Mildred, 7
New Republic, 59
New York Amsterdam News, 64
New York (city): Black public employees in, 60; Follow Through program in, 21; University of, 61; voting behavior of minorities in, 35

New York (state) University Law
    School, 66
New York Times, 36
Nixon, Richard M., xi
North Carolina: Central University
    Law School, 68; University of, 66

Oakland (Calif.), effects of Proposition
    13 in, 60
Office of Economic Opportunity, xiii,
    52; funding for, 20
Ogbu, John U., 37
Orange County (Calif.), effects of
    Proposition 13 in, 60

Packwood, Robert, 48
Packwood-Moynihan bill, 49
Paglin, Morton, 19
Panama Canal Treaty, 3
Pennsylvania, University of, 67;
    Black enrollment in the Law
    School of, 67; Law School, 66
Perkins, James A., ix
Phelps, Charles E., 80
Pittsburgh Courier, 64
Plessy v. *Ferguson,* 77, 78, 82, 83
Podhoretz, Norman, 14
*Politics and the Professors: The
    Great Society in Perspective*
    (Aaron), 23
Pontiac (Mich.), busing in, 41
Poussaint, Alvin, 64
Powell, Lewis F., 65
Progressive Era, 10
Proposition 13, xiii, 4, 57-61; and
    Black voters, 31, 59; criticism
    of, 34; and education, 60-61;
    effects of on the California public
    college and university system,
    61; and employment, 60; and
    federal spending, 57-58; and
    funding for schools, 39; and
    race, 58-59; and social services,
    59-60

Public assistance, 19
Public Opinion in America (Monroe),
    35
Public policy, trends in, x, 9
Public schools, xii, xiii; attacks on, 12,
    13, 36-40
Public Works Act of 1977, 63-64, 66
Poverty: decline in rate of, 19; defined,
    8

Rabinove, Sam, 65
Railway Mail Association v. *Corsi,* 80
Rand Corporation, 52
Raspberry, William, 65, 69
Ravitch, Diane, 42
Reconstruction Acts, 77
*Reflections on the Revolution in
    France* (Burke), 15
Regents of the University of California
    v. *Allan Bakke,* xiii, 3, 31, 63,
    64-68, 69; Black reaction to, 34;
    decision as legal precedent, 66;
    effects of decision, 66-68;
    Marshall's opinion in, 75-83
    (text); and minority admissions
    programs, 66-68; reactions to
    decision, 64-65; Supplemental
    Brief for the U.S. as *Amicus
    Curiae,* 82
Rehnquist, William H., 69
Richard Clark Associates, 30
Riesman, David, 12
Ringer, Robert J., 7
Roosevelt, Franklin D., xi, 10
Rossell, Christine, 42
Rowan, Carl, 56, 69
Rustin, Bayard, 50
Rutgers-Newark Law School, 66, 67,
    68

SALT II Treaty, 3
Samuelson, Paul, 57
Samuelson, Robert J., 58

San Diego (Calif.): Proposition 13 and education in, 61; Urban League, 43; voluntary busing in, 43; Voluntary Ethnic Enrollment Program, 43
Saulsbury, Willard, 80
Schlesinger, Arthur M., Sr., 9
Schlesinger, Arthur M., Jr., 9, 10, 11
Schooling in Capitalist America (Bowles and Gintis), 37
School tax levies and race, 38, 39
Schur, Edwin M., 7
Scopes case, 10
Simon, William E., 15, 18, 20
Simple Justice (Kluger), 75, 78
Sindler, Allan P., 65
Slaughter-House Cases, 76, 77, 80
Slave Codes, 76, 77
Slavery, 75, 76
Small Futures: Children, Inequality and the Limits of Liberal Reform (DeLone), 37
Smith, Cynthia J., x
Smith, Ralph, 67
Social Security, 19; neo-conservative attitude toward, 15
Social welfare programs, 3, 16; attacks on, 12; benefits of, 71; neo-conservative attitude toward, 17
Southern Christian Leadership Conference, 69
Sowell, Thomas, 29, 32, 34, 42, 49, 50, 51, 65
Squadron, Howard M., 65
Stand-Pat Deal, xi
Standardized tests, xiii, 54
Stanford University, 67; Hoover Institute of, 16; Medical Center, 66
The State of the Union III (Watts and Free), 6, 45
The Strange Career of Jim Crow (Woodward), 75, 77, 78
Sugarman, Stephen D., 52
Supplemental Educational Opportunity Grants, 22

Supreme Court of the United States, 46, 63, 65, 77-78, 79, 80, 81, 82
Swann v. *Charlotte-Mecklenberg Board of Education,* 81
Sweatt v. *Painter,* 79

Taggart, Robert, 21, 24
Taylor (Sen., 39th Cong.), 80
Taxation rate and government spending, 58
Tax reform, 5
Tax revolt, xiii, 4
Tocqueville, Alexis de, 15
Toledo (Ohio), school tax levies and race in, 39
Tollett, Kenneth, 64
Truman, Harry S, xi, 10, 78
Tuition tax credits, xii, xiii, 12, 42, 48-51; and Blacks, 49; Congressional attitude toward, 48-49; constitutionality of, 49; and educational opportunity, 40, 49; legislation concerning, 51; and parochial schools, 49-50; and public schools, 50; and race, 38-39; and white flight, 49-50

Unemployment, xiii; among Blacks, 6, 27, 29; Black and white compared, 28 (figure); and social and economic mobility, 37
Unemployment compensation, 19; and neo-conservatism, 15
United Jewish Organizations v. *Carey,* 81
United Negro College Fund, ix
U.S. Commission on Civil Rights, 44
U.S. Department of Commerce, Bureau of the Census, 8; Bureau of the Census, Current Population Reports, 79; Bureau of the Census, Statistical Abstract of the United States, 79

U.S. Department of Health, Education, and Welfare, 81
U.S. Department of Labor, 8, 28; Bureau of Labor Statistics, 28, 30, 31, 79
U.S. News and World Report, 27
U.S. Treasury Department, Internal Revenue Service, 8
United States v. *Cruikshank,* 79
United States v. *Reese,* 77
United Steelworkers of America v. *Weber,* xiii, 3, 63, 69–70; Black reactions to decision on, 34, 69–70; reactions to decision on, 69–70
Union of Soviet Socialist Republics, 3
Upward Bound program, 21
Uzell v. *Friday,* 66

Vietnam: refugees from, 6; war, xi, 19–20
Voting Rights Act of 1965, xi, 20

Walker Amendment, 4
Walker-Levitas Amendment, 4
Wall Street Journal, 30

War on Poverty, 18–19, 71. *See also* Great Society
Washington, University of, 65
Watergate, xi
Wattenberg, Ben, 14
Watts, William, 6, 45
Welch, Finis, 29
Welfare: The Political Economy of Welfare Reform in the United States (Anderson), 6, 19
Westinghouse Report (1969), 20
White, Byron, 65
Will, George F., 58, 65, 69
Willey, Waitman, T., 80
Williams, Walter, 29, 32, 49, 50
Willie, Charles V., 31
Wilson, James Q., 14, 17
Wilson, William Julius, 5, 31, 32, 34
Wilson, Woodrow, 78
WINning Deal, xi
Wolfe, Tom, 7
Woodward, C. Vann, 75, 77, 78

Young, Andrew, 7

Zimbabwe–Rhodesia, 3